There comes a point where a man must refuse to answer to his leader if he is also to answer to his conscience." *Sir Hartley Shawcross, Nuremberg, 1946*

"The morale, discipline and battleworthiness of the U.S. Armed Forces are, with a few salient exceptions, lower and worse than at any time in this century and possibly in the history of the United States. By every conceivable indicator, our army that now remains in Vietnam is in a state approaching collapse, with individual units avoiding or having refused combat, murdering their officers and noncommissioned officers, drug-ridden, and dispirited where not near-mutinuous." *Colonel Robert D. Heinl, Jr. "The Collapse of the Armed Forces" Armed Forces Journal, June 7, 1971*

"In retrospect, unbeknownst to me, I was part of something larger. I was operating in a vacuum, but I wasn't alone." *Alan Klein, GI Resister*

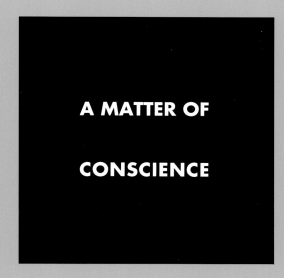

A MATTER OF

CONSCIENCE

GI Resistance During the Vietnam War

Photographs by William Short

Oral Histories by Willa Seidenberg and William Short

PAUL ATWOOD

I was born immediately after the Second World War. I always think I was born in the shadow of the bomb, and there was never a time in my childhood when I thought that men didn't go to war. My father was a perfect example of a modern day warrior, and I thought he never looked better than he did when he was in his uniform. Once I knew my father had been in the Marine Corps, I always knew that I would go in the Marine Corps someday.

When I was a kid my father kept these medals and ribbons and other Marine Corps paraphernalia in a little cigar box that he had tucked away in the back corner of his dresser. My brothers and I used to visit that little cigar box as though it were a shrine, in which these magic talismans were. I never tired of going there and opening the cover, tingling with anticipation, looking once again. I guess I saw them as badges of courage and of honor, and there was never a time in my childhood that I doubted whether I would myself wear these emblems and earn these badges.

After I refused to go to Vietnam, I wanted only to get rid of them, to forget about them, forget what they had once meant to me. I was angry at the time because, at least in that period of my life, I felt that every symbol I once valued as a symbol of something good and decent, was now in my mind a symbol of its opposite. And I think I wanted to be rid of the ties that still bound me to my father; I have to say that I wanted to be rid of his disapproval.

It's only been in the last five years or so that I've been able to pick these things up. You know, it's funny that I even have some of them. I threw virtually everything I had away, but there were some things I kept. But I never looked at them until five years ago. I began going to that little corner of my own life, one by one pulling out some things; I guess a kind of talisman again. To pick, for instance, this globe and anchor; to pick that up was like picking up something radioactive. I didn't know what it meant to me. I knew that it still meant something deep, but I was afraid of it because, even now looking at it, I get that old sense of patriotism. There's nothing wrong with love of country, but I get afraid of where that feeling leads; into a mindless, unquestioning, uncritical acceptance of policy by governmental leaders that got us involved in Vietnam in the first place.

Without exception, the people I knew who had gone to Vietnam felt they were doing something honorable. But many people would say to me it was the most fucked up thing they have ever done in their lives and wish they could get it out of their sleep, their nightmares. And in that sense, I felt I had made the right decision. I knew from listening to them that I would have been—if I survived at all—a complete basket case. I also felt convinced that my analysis of the war was correct; that it was not a self-serving one to justify my own behavior, but it was real. A more fucked up war couldn't be imagined. And it was clear to me that the Vietnam veteran was being scapegoated for the war, that collectively the United States had called upon vets to go and do something and then had turned its back on them afterwards.

STEVE FOURNIER

I volunteered to go to Vietnam. I wanted to be there, I thought it was the right thing, that we should go and protect democracy. I believed in the Domino theory and that Cardinal Spellman was right when he said, "Kill a Commie for Christ." My mother and father were both in the Navy during World War II, and there was a lot of pride in military service in my family. I was proud of being a Marine and fighting for my country.

My first night at Dong Ha I can remember being really excited looking out over the DMZ and seeing artillery fire start to walk in toward our positions, and saying, "This is wonderful, I'm really here, this is real war." The guy next to me, who had three more days left in country, was lying on the bottom of the trench begging, "God not now, just three more days, God not now!" I looked at him and thought "that's a Marine?" The next thing I knew a round blew up one of the outposts and some guys were wounded. I saw, for the first time, the effects of war.

After three months I was hit by friendly artillery fire, medevacked to Guam for recovery and shipped back to Vietnam two months later. I went on a mine sweep through Con Thien that was a real living hell; it had been defoliated, napalmed, burned and constantly shelled by both sides. The death and destruction were nothing I could have ever imagined. That was the beginning of my new look at the war. I witnessed Vietnamese torturing other Vietnamese, Marines cutting ears and penises off enemy bodies and displaying them proudly. I even saw an eight-year-old boy shot in the leg for saying, "Fuck you Marine," and an 80-year-old woman beaten by a Marine with his rifle butt.

One night during a firefight I dragged in the body of a North Vietnamese lieutenant. I thought I heard him moaning, but when I reached him I found he was dead. I searched his body; he had a scapular metal around his neck and a holy card pinned inside his shirt. The holy card looked very much like the one I had from Catholic school when I was growing up. There was a picture of himself and a young woman with a priest in front of a Cathedral—evidently in Hanoi where he was married. He was obviously a Catholic like myself, and I thought, my God, *Catholics* are involved.

After being wounded a second time, I was sent to recuperate at Chelsea Naval Hospital where I was born. With only two weeks to go before being retired from the Marines, I went to a demonstration at Boston Common. For about an hour I listened, and then I finally got up the nerve, walked to the microphone area and with my Marine haircut said, "Look, I'm just back from Vietnam and I'd like to say something." There was a bit of hesitation and then I was introduced as a Marine just returned from the war. The place got very, very quiet. I said, "I just wanted to tell you that myself and some other Marines have been calling you people back here in The World a lot of lousy names and claiming that we'd like to do some terrible things to you and well . . . I want to apologize. I think you're doing something wonderful for America and I'm proud to be here with you today." I got a wonderful ovation. I felt like, God, I'm home, I'm *finally home.*

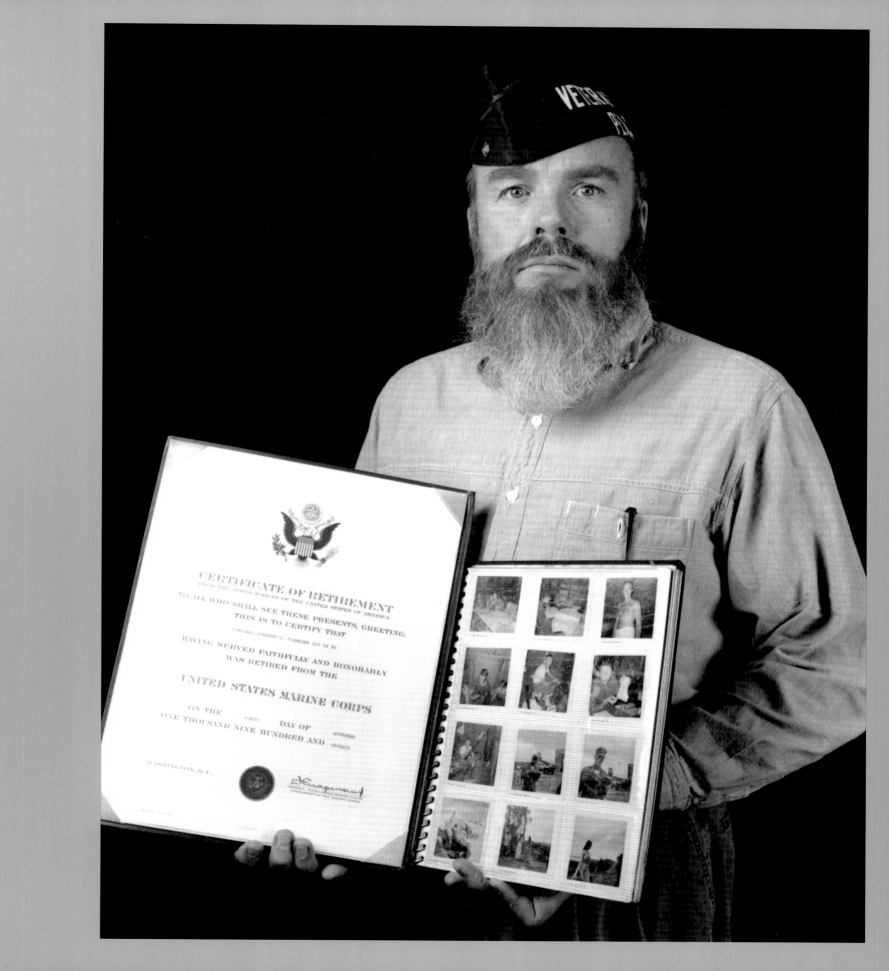

BILL SHORT

I served with the Blue Spaders 1 BN 26 INF First Infantry Divsion, otherwise known as the "Bloody Red One" from February, 1969 to July, 1969. I was an infantry platoon sergeant with Mike platoon in Alpha Company. My tour of duty was cut short by my own volition.

My unit patrolled the Michelin rubber plantation, operating in company strength by day and splitting up into platoon-size ambushes for the night. We usually spent three to five days doing this before we rested in a fire support base for a couple of days. Whenever we made contact or blew an ambush the body count came next. I would never view the bodies, I was afraid to. I didn't want to know what I was doing. So when the guys would say, "Hey Sarge, we got to check out the dead gooks," I always made up some excuse. I knew it was my responsibility as platoon sergeant to be on top of all situations, but somehow the body count was something I had no desire to be part of. After a firefight I felt drained and empty, it seemed pointless. Our battles were never decisive and tomorrow always came with the welcome of surviving one day only to have to face another. The last thing I wanted to do was count bloody body parts so we could compete with the Second of the Twenty-eight, the Black Lions, our sister battalion, for first place in the division.

I carried my weapon and fired many rounds through it, but I always felt protected against taking another life because twenty or eighty other guys fired too. For years after the war, when people would ask the inevitable question, "did you kill anyone?" I always answered I don't know, but in reality I did.

On one company-size operation we broke for a rest at midday. My RTO, because he had a feeling, put his claymore mine out, something we only did for ambush. Halfway through our lunch all hell broke loose. Barney blew his claymore, and after a three-hour firefight things were calm again. The attack came from three Viet Cong, two of whom we got. When the body count came I went for the first time to see the remains. Both VC had been killed by the blast from one of our grenades, and as I approached the first thing I noticed was a piece of bone protruding from the hand of one of the bodies. It seemed to glow white hot, I thought it was the brightest thing I had ever seen. The next thing I noticed was how heavy the body seemed to my eyes. It looked as if it were glued to the ground.

One of the new NCOs, a staff sergeant and second timer, decided we should booby trap the bodies and he asked for my help. We rolled them over and pulled the secondary pins on two grenades leaving the primary detonation lever in place. Each grenade was placed, lever side up and under the rib cage beneath the dead men. Later that night, while positioned in a company-size ambush, I heard the grenades go off. I knew the comrades of the men we had killed had come to claim the bodies and quite possibly had gotten something extra to go with their grief. I *knew* I was responsible for taking human life. Two months later I refused to go out on any more combat missions.

CLARENCE FITCH

My father was in the military in World War II, and even though he was in a segregated army, it was very much a part of his life experience. Being a veteran wasn't something that was looked down on; it was one of the few things black men had that they could hold up as being honorable, as being accepted, as being proof that you had just as much right to anything that was going to be given out, even though you didn't get it all the time. That's why a lot of the hostility and resentment came, because they didn't get their just due. But they did get some things out of it. My father went to mechanics school on the GI bill. The house my mother lives in right now was bought on the GI bill. We probably would not have been able to do it without the GI bill. My father talked about his personal experiences in the war all the time. I could tell you where he was stationed because he told us a thousand times. He made us sit down and listen to the stories, but he didn't really elaborate on the negatives and the racism.

For me and other black GIs in Vietnam in 1967, things were changing. Things going on in the States affected our behavior there. Some of the same black consciousness, the whole black power movement, was taking place there too. We were growing Afros, expressing ourselves through ritualistic handshakes, black power handshakes, African beads, hanging around in cliques, trying to eat up as much of the black music as we could get our hands on. We kind of segregated ourselves; we didn't want to integrate into what we considered the white man's war. For the first time I was looking at the enemy, not so much as the enemy, but as another minority, brown people. The North Vietnamese reminded us of it too.

People started really trying to educate themselves about how the war started, where the war was going. We read a lot of the books, *Confessions of Nat Turner*, *Soul On Ice*, all of the black publications, *Ebony*, *Jet*, as much as we could see because we wanted to be a part of it. There were some nights we had 20, 30, 50 brothers hanging out. When we went into a mess hall we ate together in certain parts of the mess hall. They were trying to make us get haircuts, cut those Afros off, and people were going to jail to keep their hair. We tried to spend almost all of our time together, the "Bloods" in Vietnam, we tried to have all black hooches. The brass would try to prevent this, they would try to assign us to integrated hooches and stuff like that.

When I was put in the brig, it was like another awareness. Because the brig was like, there were white Marines in the brig, but the overwhelming majority were black, much like the jails were back in The World. It just made you more bitter, more conscious, more hard, more militant, gave you more of a reason for being what you were and to resist and to fight, and make sure you educated yourself and educated others.

You laid down at night and there was just so much tension going through you, with all the racial stuff, the war itself and we were so young. But it felt like we were so much older. It felt like you had lived a long time. That year in Vietnam was like 20 years, you saw so much and witnessed so much.

SUSAN SCHNALL

My father was killed during the Second World War, in 1945 on Guam in the Pacific. He died a hero. They landed on the beachhead and he went back a number of times, even though he was wounded, to save the men under his command. It practically destroyed my mother when he was killed. She terribly resented the military for taking him. That's the image of war and the military I grew up with and because of that I had a very personal involvement against war and against suffering.

When I went for my Navy physical I wore a peace necklace and I remember the doctor asking me why I was wearing it. I said, "Because I'm against war." The recruiter told me if I were ever in Vietnam and there was a Vietnamese soldier who needed to be taken care of, I could take care of that person. So there was not supposed to be any problem being against war. My rationalization for going into the Navy was to undo the damage the United States was doing abroad. These young kids were sent overseas and shot up; they needed good care, and that's what I was going to do. But there was a point at which it was obvious that I had to do something about the war, that I was no longer patching up people to feel better, but that I was promoting the war machine.

In 1968 I heard about the GI and Veterans March for Peace in San Francisco for October 12th. I went to the meetings, and got posters and leaflets and put them up on base at the Oak Knoll Naval Hospital, where I was stationed. We put posters up in the middle of the night and within an hour they were all down. I remembered hearing about B-52 bombers dropping leaflets on the Vietnamese, urging them to defect. I thought if the United States can do that in Vietnam, then why can't I do it here. A Vietnam vet, a friend who was a pilot, my husband and I loaded up the airplane with those leaflets promoting the peace march.

We loaded up the plane and the press was called to expect us over various areas in the San Francisco Bay area. We made a couple of trial runs; one didn't turn out so well. At a couple of thousand feet up, we opened the door of the airplane to let the leaflets out and the plane dropped about a thousand feet! So we reloaded the plane and went back. We hit the Presidio, Oak Knoll Naval Hospital, Treasure Island, Yerba Buena Island, the deck of the USS Enterprise. Then we landed and held a press conference and I said, "I did it." The press asked me to go back in the airplane and get out again, so they'd have good footage. And they did an interview. The military used all of the footage at my court martial—evidence I really was guilty.

That was Thursday and the March for Peace was on Saturday. I wore my uniform in the demonstration that I was told specifically not to do. A general Navy regulation stated you can't wear your uniform when you're speaking religious, partisan, political views publicly. I thought, if General Westmoreland can wear his uniform before Congress asking for money for Vietnam, I can wear mine as a member of the Armed Forces speaking out against the war. I had as much right to freedom of speech as he does. I gave a speech and I knew when I got up to the microphones, one of these belongs to the Navy. But it didn't make any difference.

STEVE SPUND

I told my family I was on 30-day leave. But after 30 days were up, my father became suspicious and knew something was wrong. A short time after the 30-day period I was awakened by the police. My father had called the police and reported me.

They took me to this compound at the Brooklyn Navy Yard with barbed wire fence, jagged glass on top of the high walls and one main door in the front with Marine guards at the door. They asked me if I would consent to going back. I said sure. I probably would have said anything to get out of the Marine barracks at that point. So, remarkably enough, they gave me a bus ticket and told me to go back to North Carolina. I didn't go back, I went home to my parents' house, hoping for more time to think of something. It wasn't too long later before my father turned me in again. This time the MPs came.

They took me to the Naval Brig and I started to get worked over by the Marine guards. You'd be stripped of all your clothing, they take your unmentionables and put them through the bars and hit them or stretch them or choke you until you're white, or out of air. They usually tried to do things that would not leave bruises or blood. They called you the lowest thing on earth, but not just terms that they might use in boot camp to break you down. This was of a personal nature to them, 'cause usually these Marine guards had done at least one tour of duty in Vietnam and they'd seen a lot of their buddies die. To them you were the worst thing on earth.

Two of these guards told me this was my last weekend, that they were going to kill me. I checked around with other prisoners and quite a few of them told me that the guards had hung a few marines and made it look like suicide. I couldn't believe at first that anyone would do that to another American, or another Marine. But they assured me it was so, and at that point, I wasn't going to take any chances. I started to believe that they'd sooner see me dead at their hands than free at mine.

I was faced with another tough choice. One was going back to North Carolina and then to Vietnam, or take my own life. I decided that was the right thing to do. They took us to the PX to get a shave kit and all that other kind of stuff. They were supposed to take out the blades from the shave kits, but the guards were busy and I took the moment to put a package of blades in my pockets. There was one Marine guard that wasn't crazy like these other two and I told him if he could to get in touch with the chaplain or the rabbi, I wanted last rites. He came back and said they were both unavailable and for awhile I felt that this was it, I was going to do it 'cause the next day the other guards were coming back on duty. Unexpectedly a visiting psychiatrist heard what I was up to. He came in and saw my condition and knew I was going to do it. He sent me to St. Albans Hospital in Queens for observation in the psychiatric ward.

I received a general discharge with honorable conditions at the Brooklyn Navy Yard. I thought it was strange, not only to be back there again, but the sergeant asked me—and he was serious—if I would like to enlist again. I don't remember the vulgarity I used, but I'm sure I let him know that I wasn't interested.

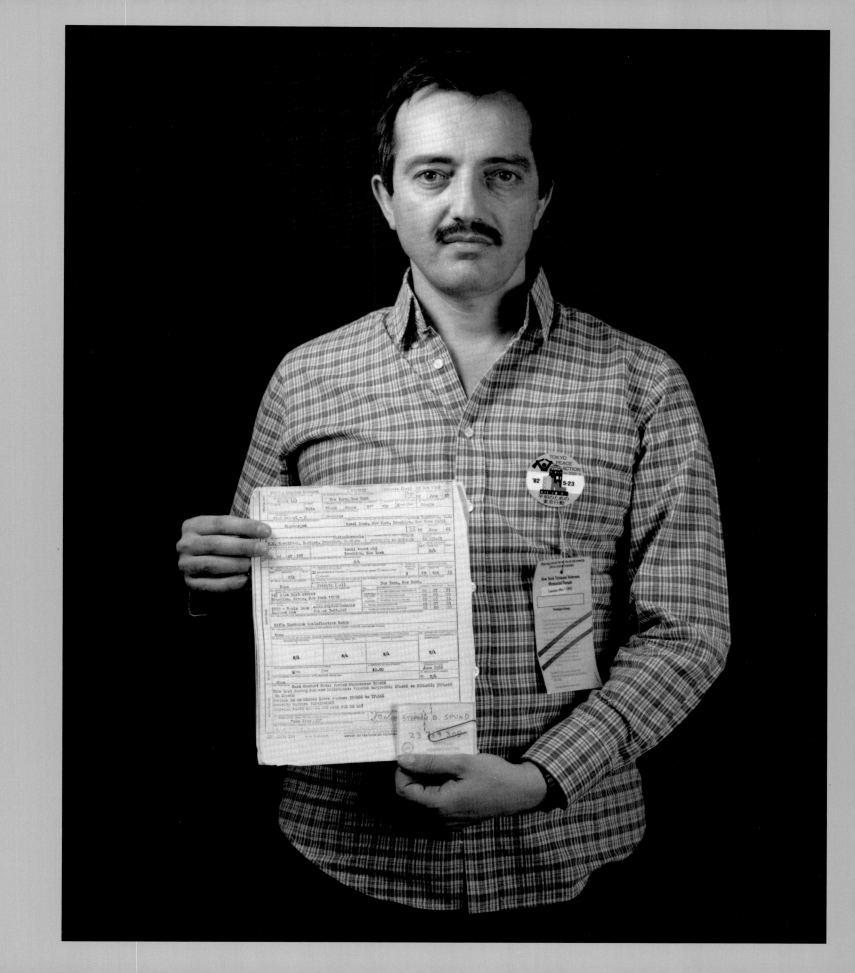

MIKE WONG

I was born and raised in San Francisco, in the Polk District, which at that time was mostly a Chinese district. The Chinese have a real different slant on war. They see it as one of the miseries of life that comes around periodically, like famines, and it was never glamorized. In Chinese society the hierarchy was nobles at the top, scholars directly under them, farmers, then merchants and last of all soldiers.

I got my draft notice in 1968. I didn't know what to do. I was no longer convinced the war was right, but I wasn't totally convinced it was wrong either. I finally decided I would volunteer in order to get into the medics. One time we were in the line for the mess hall, a real long line. We could see people whispering to each other and passing it down. And when the whisper got to me, the guy in front of me said, "They're killing women and children in Vietnam." I said, "Who's killing women and children? The Viet Cong?" And he said, "No, we are." When we got to the front we saw this newspaper rack with pictures of My Lai on the front pages. I can't describe what that did to us. There could no longer be any doubt as to who's right and who's wrong.

I received orders for Vietnam and decided to go AWOL and then turn myself into the Presidio Stockade, plead guilty to AWOL and then they'd have to throw me in the stockade. That would become my permanent duty station and I could apply for CO. They had me in the stockade for like 20 minutes and a guard comes and pulls me back in the office. This lieutenant wants me to sign this thing saying they're releasing me from the stockade and putting me back on Vietnam orders, and I was to proceed immediately to Oakland Army Terminal for shipment to Vietnam. My lawyer says, just sign it. So they released me and my lawyer took me back to his office and said, "They were going to stick a gun in your face and put handcuffs on you and then put you on the plane. I managed to talk them into releasing you into my custody. My legal responsibility is to take you to Oakland Army Terminal. If you resist, of course, you're a trained soldier, I can't very well stop you." I was so young and naive, I had no idea what to do. I finally got the hint and I split.

I knew Canada was my only remaining option. But to go to Canada was to desert, to run away, to say I'm a coward. I was just going around and around in circles. So I went to this Chinese movie theater to stop thinking about it. What was showing was a movie about Chinese guerrillas fighting the Japanese during World War II. I came out and realized I only had two choices: either I could go to Vietnam and do to the Vietnamese what the Japanese had done to the Chinese in World War II, or I could go to Canada. The question had been framed in black and white: do you want to be a murderer or do you want to be a coward? And I finally decided that the worst thing that can happen with a coward is he hurts himself, but a murderer not only hurts himself, he hurts other people too. And so I went to Canada.

People think we make these decisions lightly and that all the people that went to Canada just ran away. I was prepared to go to prison and fight my case for as long as the war lasted. Going to Canada was the hardest decision of my life. It was questions of manhood, giving up your family, your country, your friends, giving up everything you knew. I went to Canada with the assumption I would be there for the rest of my life, that I would be an exile, a criminal, wanted by the FBI . . . and that I could never come home again.

HOWARD LEVY

I was part of a plan whereby doctors could defer being called into the Army to allow them to finish whatever specialty training they were doing. I really didn't want to go into the military. It just seemed that since they were drafting young doctors, I was going to go whether I liked it or not, so I might as well go on my terms. At the time I made the commitment the war in Vietnam was just a little blip. As the war began to escalate, and my time to go began to draw near, which was in '65, my opinion about the war changed drastically. By now there was no question where I was coming from with regard to Vietnam. The only question was, what the hell do I do about it? I went into the Army figuring number one, I'll buy time. Number two, I worked it out so I would be sent down South, where I figured I could at least do some civil rights work that I'd been wanting to do anyhow. And number three, I figured I'll draw the line somewhere. I knew where that was going to be—when they ordered me to go to Vietnam.

I was stationed at Fort Jackson, South Carolina, where I ran a clinic, and every night and on weekends I would go to the town of Prosperity to work with an organization that was registering blacks to vote. At some point the Army assigned some Green Beret guys to me and I was supposed to train them in some aspect of dermatology. I did that for a number of months, which really allowed me to get to know them. The more I got to know them, the more upsetting some of their stories became. I reached a point when I just said, "Look, I've figured this out and I can't train you guys anymore." I said, "I don't really want you in the clinic, so let's not make a big fuss about it, but I want you to leave." And they did. Each month a new guy would come and I'd give him the same spiel. That went on for a number of months.

By the time charges were brought against me, I only had another two or three months in the Army. It turns out from the trial testimony that Military Intelligence knew of my activities within days, maybe hours of me arriving in Prosperity. But actually they had been tracing me from my days when I was involved in some Socialist Worker Party stuff, before I went in the Army. My CO was only going to give me a slap on the wrist until they threw the intelligence report on his desk which detailed the fact that I was a fucking Communist. That's basically what it said. He then decided it was going to be court-martial.

We tried to put the war on trial, but the military court said the truth is no defense. Another defense we used was medical ethics, saying the real objection to training the Green Berets is that they were using medicine as just another propaganda tool. If you had a bunch of kids in a poor village in Vietnam, and you gave them a shot of penicillin and cured them of their impetigo and suddenly they looked much healthier and didn't have ugly skin things all over their bodies, you would probably make some friends in town. That strikes me as illegitimate because it can be taken away as easily as it can be given. That's not a basis for doing medicine. I was sentenced to three years in Leavenworth. The only shock was . . . it wasn't nine.

PETER HAGERTY

In the summer of 1970 I spent eight weeks in Vietnam as an activist for GI rights with the Lawyers Military Defense Committee. My job was to go out into the field and let servicemen know legal counsel was available. I hitched rides everywhere I could, on convoys and in C-130's, any way to anywhere; up Highway 1, Da Nang, Hue, the DMZ, up the Perfume River, Saigon and the Delta. I felt like a fish out of water. Here I was a ponytailed civilian in jungle fatigues running around Vietnam looking for servicemen in trouble.

I became involved with GI rights after I was released from the Navy. I entered Naval ROTC in my junior year at Harvard University. Two days before graduation I made it known I was thinking about refusing my commission. I was given a visitor pass to Kittery Naval Brig and told to take a look because if I didn't accept this commission that was where I would be spending a lot of time. So, after some compromising on the Navy's part and mine, I decided to enter the service. At my last duty station I was in charge of the forward guns on a destroyer preparing for assignment in the Gulf of Tonkin. I discovered some hairline cracks in the barrels, reported it and was ordered to OK them anyway. I refused, and further refused any duty in Vietnam. I later learned the guns did explode and killed seven men, including the officer in charge.

I think my involvement in GI rights and my desire to go to Vietnam after I fought so hard to stay out, in part, grew out of the action I took in the service, and a sense of class guilt. I received no punishment for my actions because I was an officer and had gone to a prestigious university.

I grew up in a small New England town in the 50's and I remember the McCarthy era; hiding under my desk in elementary school as Russian bombers supposedly flew overhead. I had a profound image of what Communism was and I feared Communists, even though I was against U.S. involvement in Vietnam.

I came face to face with the "evil" from my childhood on one of my sojourns in Vietnam. I went on an interview with a French camera crew to a banana-shaped island in the middle of the Mekong River. We were interviewing a famous monk referred to as the Coconut Monk. On the second night we were there, at about two o'clock in the morning, I heard a small motor boat pull up and dock. I watched as eight or ten guys in black pajamas walked up the path toward me. They came up to me, saw my American fatigues and ponytail, and didn't flinch at all. Speaking in French, they asked if I was American and I asked who they were. They looked at each other, smiled and answered they were NVA. I froze with fear, but to my surprise, one for them asked in English how the Yankees were doing. It was great, it just broke the ice. Unfortunately, I was not a baseball fan and could not help them out. We sat around for two or three hours talking; these guys crowding around me, fascinated about American life. I learned they were on R&R and had traveled by river at night all the way from northern Laos, at great risk to their own lives, just to have a religious experience with this monk. That was the first time I met the "enemy."

GREG PAYTON

I was in a supply unit in Vietnam located in Long Binh. We went out on the field depot and I worked a location deck. What they told us was, if we come in and do the right thing in the beginning, that we're doing the menial jobs now and as other groups come in they will get the jobs and we will get a better situation. So I accepted that for words. So in the beginning we had a lot of dirty jobs: burning feces, cleaning out urine pits and all kind of different things. But what I began to notice is that a lot of white recruits were coming in and they weren't getting the same assignments I was getting. It seemed like we were always pulling up the short end of the stick.

One time the first sergeant was talking about these gooks or something, and I replied . . . "*yeah, the gook is the same thing as a nigger.*" It was like a light went off, it was a real revelation. I was naive about a lot of things. I had to develop a racist attitude. I never was raised with that. The first sergeant told me I was a *smart nigger,* that's just what he said.

One incident that really opened my eyes was with a white GI named Muncey, from Kentucky. He was really a typical super artificial macho guy. A group of Vietnamese kids came up to our truck as we were coming back from guard duty. We had food and stuff and we'd feed the people out in the field. We had leftover food, bushels of apples and oranges and stuff. These kids came up to the truck begging and you could see it in their faces, these kids had that *I'm hungry, feed me*, kind of look. So Muncey says look at these gook kids and he took a bite out of an apple and threw it in the dirt and about four or five kids dove on it. It was just like when you drop a piece of bread in the fish tank. It just really set me off. I damn near threw him out of the truck and it was still moving. I was brought up on charges for that.

I had three courts-martial and I went to the stockade and it was all these black people . . . all these brothers. That blew my mind. After I'd been in the stockade about two months, I made it to minimum-security and I had a work detail. I used to bring in kerosene to burn the feces with. Some guys got together and said they were going to have a riot in the stockade. They asked me to bring in an extra can of kerosene every other day so they couldn't see build-up. So I did. It started in minimum-security but they went to maximum-security and broke the locks and let everybody out. They picked noon because that's when the guards change and most of them were eating in the mess hall. They broke the gate, broke the lock, let everybody out of maximum security, and started burning the hooches and what not. There was a lot of chaos. A lot of people got hurt and I imagine some people got killed. I remember seeing white guys, in particular, and guards getting beat up with bunk adapters. If you were white you were in trouble, whether you were a good guy or a bad guy.

I've never been as violent as I was in Vietnam. There was a lot of rage; it just began to build and build. I did so many things that were unnecessary and hurt some people and it really wasn't their fault. But I had to take it out somewhere, I had to vent this anger in some way. Today I work on not becoming violent, I'm scared of violence.

JOHN TUMA

At my first duty station in Vietnam, a Military Intelligence detachment, I refused to work with South Vietnamese interpreters who were using physical coercion in order to extract "the truth" from North Vietnamese and Viet Cong soldiers. There were four or five ARVN interpreters who were working with the Military Intelligence unit. And although I was language-trained in Vietnamese, it was standard operational procedure to have a Vietnamese interpreter with Americans in order to make sure no nuances of the language escaped any one and maybe to check up on us.

The first person I was to interrogate was an NVA soldier who had been brought in during Operation Iron Mountain. I started doing basic debriefing of the individual and realized that the Vietnamese interpreter was pulling and twisting on the man's ear lobe and had it stretched down somewhere below his chin line. I told him to stop, and he did, only to start again after a few moments. I stopped the questioning and requested another Vietnamese interpreter and the same thing happened. I decided to end the debriefing session.

My next interrogation was of a suspected Viet Cong who had been shot. He was from a small village on the Laotian border. We had nothing that showed he had ever been a Viet Cong and I classified him as being civilian, possibly civilian defendant. The South Vietnamese I was working with to debrief the fellow, kept pinching off his IV (intravenous) tubes while we were talking. I told him several times to stop, but it was totally out of my control. I tried using three other Vietnamese interpreters after that and they also abused the prisoner; either cutting off his IV or pulling and twisting on his ear lobe or twisting a handful of flesh from his side in order to create pain. I refused to work with them.

As a result, I was transferred out of the MI detachment. I was later asked to interpret at the evacuation of a refugee camp and was sent in unarmed to an area with several South Vietnamese from the Province Recon Unit. I felt something was wrong . . . very, very wrong. I was told we were looking for a woman and some children who were supposed to be on the farthest edge of the village. We got to village edge and they told me it was just a little farther. We went through the tree line, and still farther. I realized they were acting very nervous and suspicious. They ran forward to a small ravine and I started running back. When I got to the edge of the village I heard gunfire behind me. The fire was directed at me; they were not supposed to bring me back alive. Earlier I had reported the use of a "birdcage" (a cage constructed of barbed wire wrapped around a captive and then hung in a tree) in a Vietnamese compound and they were forced to take it down. Shortly after this incident my hooch was fragged with a percussion grenade.

I was threatened with court-martial several times, but I always thought about what would my parents have done. What would be the right thing to do, not from the Army's point of view, but from my family's and my community's. I consciously thought about that and came to the conclusion there were things I had been raised not to do and couldn't and wouldn't do.

CHARLIE CLEMENTS

I grew up on military bases because my father was in the Air Force, and I suppose I was groomed from the time I was a little boy to go into the Air Force. My brother went to the Air Force Academy and I followed. At the Academy we were instilled with a tremendous sense of duty and discipline, and of honor and ethics; a theme that one dealt with almost everyday there because one could take a pencil from somebody else and if you didn't return it, that was considered an honor violation and you would have to turn yourself in and leave the Academy. It was a black and white world. I think it was that sense of honor that probably lead me to my refusal to fly anymore in Vietnam.

I entered pilot training with the clear understanding that I didn't want to kill anybody, but I can't tell you why I felt that way. I trained in a C-130, then went to Vietnam and slowly began to see things differently. I began to have a real revulsion about what was going on, but I never thought about quitting.

I flew a secret mission to Cambodia and I remember looking out of the plane and seeing vast areas that looked like the moon. Only one thing did that: B-52's. I realized we were conducting massive bombing operations there. We began ferrying troops from Saigon to Parrot's Beak, positioning troops for an invasion. I was furious. I had a cold so I declared myself unfit to fly.

I went off to California for a few days and went to an anti-war rally at San Francisco State with a friend. I felt, *this is it, I'm not going to go back, I'm not going to fly any more missions*. Somehow the organizers got me to speak and I just told people, "I'm a lieutenant in the Air Force and I'm not going to fly any more. I've seen a lot of terrible things and I'm saying *no*."

I went back to Vietnam and asked for a transfer to a unit that didn't have anything to do with Vietnam. Some months later I got a call to go to San Antonio where I saw this Air Force psychiatrist. He said, "Don't worry Clements, we'll have you back in Saigon in a week, you're in the old three-year slump." I said, "You're pretty fucked up if you think I'm going back." I talked about the Phoenix program, about secret bases in Laos, about flying plane loads of money down there for this black marketing scam, about secret missions into Cambodia, and coups and invasions and I think he thought I was totally whacked.

He gave me an envelope and sent me across town to some place. I went across town, gave them this envelope and they gave me a pair of pajamas. I had gone in the back door of a psychiatric ward and there I was! I couldn't make any telephone calls, I couldn't have any visitors, and I was given medications. If I didn't take the medication I was told I would be strapped down and injected. I didn't know if I was crazy or not, but I was beginning to think so because the nurses and doctors were intelligent, educated people, and they were treating me like I was one of the other patients. Then the major from across town came and said that if I would agree to go back to Saigon they would drop all this psychiatric stuff. That was a turning point for me because I knew if I was crazy, I was crazy because I chose to be. Soon after, a friend of mine kind of broke into the ward. We were supposed to have dinner the night I had disappeared and he finally found me.

ALAN KLEIN

I was born in Germany in 1946 to parents who were survivors of the camps. All my relatives were victims of World War II. The ideas I had about war were maybe different than what an average American kid had because I grew up thinking it was my lot to go into the camps, just as it might have been the lot of a normal kid to go into the military. I remember being real small, my eyes were tabletop level, and I would watch my father and his friends playing cards, and all of them had the numbers tattooed on their arms. They would deal cards and tell stories about how they survived. And that's what I thought I would do.

The very same day I got my draft notice I went to the Air Force recruiter and enlisted. On one of my trips home I was in O'Hare Airport waiting on military stand-by. This guy comes by and he's got his hand right on the counter, this doughy, pudgy hand, all pinkish. I glanced up his sleeve and saw that patch: Airborne. And then I looked up at his face. He had been burned and he was all puffy. And it was only when we started talking that I realized he was black. It was in his voice; he was from Yazoo, Mississippi. I was just dumbstruck. What got me most was that he was 17 and I couldn't tell his age and I couldn't tell his color. He had been denuded of that. I went home depressed about that. My father met me and he was telling me about a big killing he made on the stock market with a munitions company. Suddenly it became crystal clear. It was a bolt of lightning. I said, *he's* the one who should have been in that young guy's place—he has a real reason to fight, he needs the war to make money. Those are the guys that ought to be fighting this war, not that kid. And certainly not me.

From that point on, it was never the same again. I came back and announced to my friends, from here on in I'm opposed to the war and I'm going to fuck up this place as bad as I can. I'm not going to Vietnam, but I'm not going to be sitting around doing nothing either. We decided what we could best do is destroy the efficiency of our outfit.

Everything we touched was no longer assumed to be used to further the efficiency of the U.S. military. Everything we did was designed to be messed up, sabotaged, or basically deemed done by incompetents, and thereby they would exert more energy to keep us in line and less to wage war. So little by little, it might be a truck that was neglected, it might be the tip of a wing that was damaged, just anything to keep it off-balance.

Finally, in the fall of '66 a group of us decided we would go AWOL. We got back and turned ourselves over to our officer and he said, "If you promise not to leave, we will just confine you to barracks." The other guys said, "Absolutely." I said, "Fuck you, not only do I promise not to leave, I'm gonna leave right now." That was the end of it, I was in jail.

Just before I was released I heard the reason I was being let out was because we got this directive that said all the people who committed the following offenses would hereby be dismissed and at present rank. So it dawned on me, and somebody else told us, there were thousands and thousands of guys who were doing time, costing the military a lot of money. It's really interesting in retrospect to think that, unbeknownst to me, I was part of something larger. I was operating in a vacuum, but I wasn't alone. Rather than feeling anonymous, I found tremendous solace in subsequently knowing there were so many other people who were as ill-formed as I, groping along trying to find their way, and reacting to anger and fear, but all of us, in our own way coming to the same point.

DAVE BLALOCK

One night we were sitting around the barracks in Vietnam getting high and smoking dope and passing around this full page ad in *The New York Times* that a guy who had just come back from R&R in Hawaii had clipped out. Everybody's reading and saying, "Wow, this is great, this is really neat . . . why don't we do something on this date, November 15th." We only had two days to do anything. We came to a decision that we're going to wear black arm bands and we're going to refuse to go out on patrol. And then some other guys said, "Why don't we spread this to these other units, to the engineers, to the 1st Cav guys and everyone else in our camp."

The next day we went around to all of our friends and contacts in the other units and put out the word—what do you guys think of this thing, we want to do this, we want to shut the whole base camp down on that day. The word spread and it seemed like everybody was going to do it, but we weren't sure. I remember the night before the 15th we were up all night long, wondering what they're going to do or what's going to happen with the 1st Cav guys, trying to assess what was going to happen, how successful we were going to be. Finally we fell asleep. There was a little MP detachment on our camp, these were dog handlers. The MPs ran the PA system and they played the morning taps—military music—in the morning over the PA system. The morning of the 15th we wake up at about five in the morning, and instead of playing the military shit, they put Jimi Hendrix's *Star Spangled Banner* on. And nobody even told the MPs about this thing! These guys were obviously into it also.

So we went in morning formation with our new commanding officer. The former CO was blown away six weeks earlier—he was killed, fragged. The new CO was pretty slick and all the officers were afraid of us at that point. So we went out in morning formation and

we're all wearing black arm bands. It was like 100 percent of the enlisted men, everybody's wearing a black arm band, including some of the war doctors and the helicopter pilots. The CO comes out and he says, "I'll tell you what we're going to do today, you guys. I think we're going to give you guys a day off." He was real slick with it.

So then we jumped in a jeep and cruised around the perimeter to the other units to find out what was happening, whether they were going to be successful. The engineers were in formation. We pulled up on the edge of their company area and their CO had pulled—he knew who the leaders of the thing were—them out of the ranks and threatened to shoot them on the spot unless they took their black arm bands off and anybody that refused to go out and do their duty for the day would be shot for mutiny. Whether they'd do it or not is another story, but that intimidated a lot of the other people because only 50 percent of the engineers were wearing black arm bands. But they ended up not doing any duty anyway because a guy sabotaged all the bulldozers and everything, and nothing worked. So they couldn't do anything.

Anyway, that was the influence of a full-page ad in *The New York Times*. Somebody saw that and gave us the opportunity to do something bigger than just killing an officer or something like that.

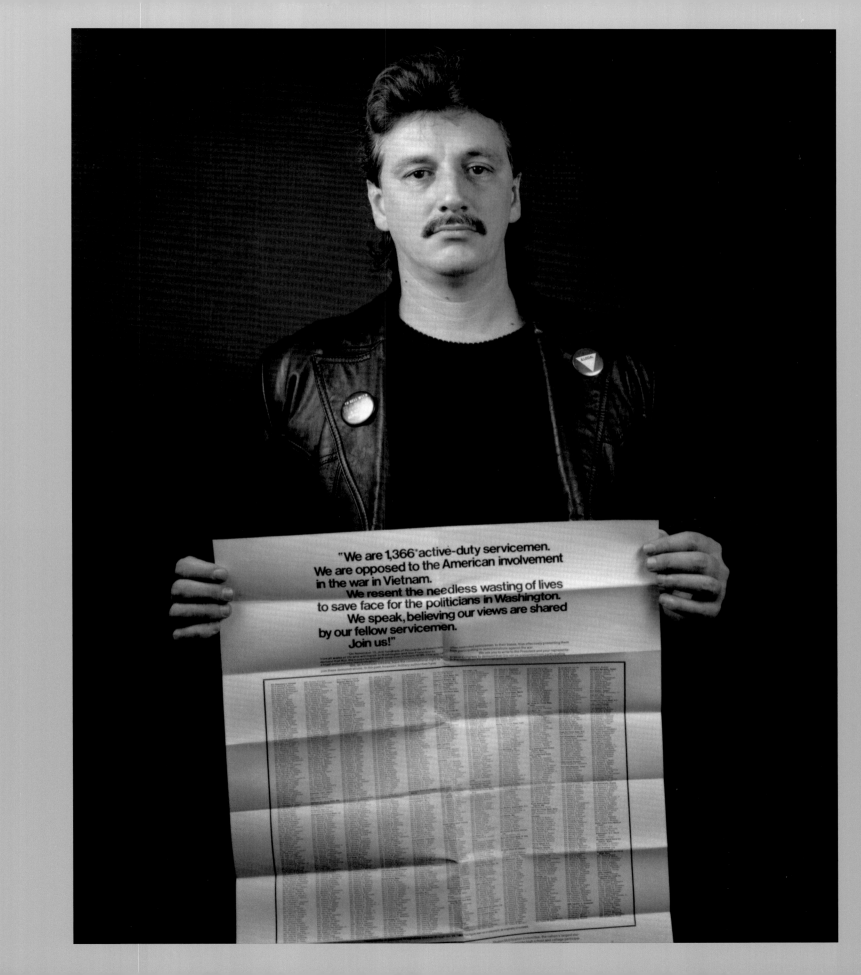

ANDY STAPP

In 1965 four of us burned our draft cards and got booted out of Penn State. I remember feeling that the U.S. was committing war crimes and a draft card was like a South African pass card by the very fact they said you could get five years in jail for burning it . . . a piece of paper. I wanted to go in the Army—to organize it.

At some point in training the Army figured out I had burned my draft card and was a left-wing radical. They thought I should have my own room, but they couldn't give a private his own room. That's only for officers. You just can't isolate somebody in the Army, it's all collective labor. So they put guys around me they thought were the most Army type. Well, they were just the first two guys won over. And together we had a lot of success in the barracks, putting up anti-war literature everywhere. So much so that the Army went after us to stop it. They figured out all the literature was in this foot locker of mine. This lieutenant came in, took the lock off, and when I came out of the bathroom he was going to order me to empty the locker. Well, another guy saw what happened, and he went and put his lock on it while the lieutenant's back was turned. And they got this sergeant—who was very anti-war, I knew him well—and this colonel says, "Chop open his locker." And right in front of the colonel, this sergeant looked over at me like, should I chop it open, is it okay with you? And I say, go ahead, it's all right. So I was court-martialed for that, disobeying a direct order to open the locker.

I got in touch with the Emergency Civil Liberties Committee. ECLC was set up in the 1950's because the ACLU wouldn't defend communists. ECLC sent out a shotgun press release about the court-martial that went to every left-wing group in the country. So a whole bunch of radicals descended on Fort Sill, just to make the Army's life even more hellish.

The battalion I was in was ordered to Vietnam without me. I just got transferred to another unit. They transferred me a lot. I was court-martialed again and acquitted. So then the Army just said, *we'll charge him with treason; causing or attempting to cause insubordination, disloyalty and refusal to duty among members of the Armed Forces.* The trial was on the first day of the Tet Offensive. I remember picking up the paper and seeing that 60 towns were attacked.

It took about two months to really get the trial going. In the meantime we began putting out a newspaper called *The Bond.* And during Christmas leave I came up to New York and met GIs from nine different bases, and we set up the American Servicemen's Union. We had ten demands: an end of racism in the Army; the right to refuse illegal orders, like to go fight in Vietnam; rank and file control of court-martial boards; end of saluting and sir-ing of officers; no troops against anti-war demonstrators; right of free political association. Over a five-year period the ASU had 20,000 members, but not more than 10,000 at once. We had ASU chapters on about 100 installations in the U.S. and about 60 ships.

Whatever the verdict was in my treason trial was secret, but it goes up higher to see if it's confirmed or not. And then I was discharged with about two weeks left to go. This lieutenant drove me to the gate, and he said, "I am happy Private, and I'll tell you why I'm happy—because I get to be the guy that tells General Brown that you're no longer in the Army." He was laughing and he said, "I want to tell you if you step one foot back on this base from this moment, you'll get six months in prison."

Basic training was really brutal and rude. It kind of shocked me, and the inhumanity of it reinforced my doubts about war. Just to survive the day-to-day routine, I suppressed my anti-war feelings for a period of several months. The training reality is so intense around you that it doesn't leave room for much else. I got an ulcer when I was going through Special Forces medical training. I sat down with myself and said, I think you know what this ulcer's about. I had, in a sense, become a little schizophrenic. I told myself, you're going to have to decide who you are and who you're going to be. So I fenagled a leave back to the San Francisco Bay area. I sat down in the backyard of my home and wrote this long, dramatic letter to the papers and had my picture in both papers. *The Chronicle* said, "Anti-war Green Beret Drops Out." I went back to Fort Bragg to face the music. I went through about six months of pretrial legal maneuverings, and realized they were going to make an example of me. Eventually they convicted me of two counts of refusing orders to go to Vietnam, and sentenced me to ten years in prison. But I wasn't present at my court-martial. I had already deserted—I decided my freedom was more important than I thought.

I got a passport sent to me in Canada, which was really a godsend. After a couple of months I decided to go to Europe. I lived in Germany for six months and I was totally broke, so of course I called home. My mom told me the FBI had been there the day before and for the first time they got her goat, which is great because my father was a cop and she's used to cooperating with the system. The first couple of times they had Navy Intelligence visit her and she said, "Oh, they were such nice young men." But this time they called her a liar because they couldn't get the information from her they wanted, because she didn't have it. So I just happened to call the next day and she says, "They know where you are, they're getting closer." I'd been postponing doing the obvious thing of going to Sweden. I arrived in Sweden in November of '69, the day of the first snowfall there.

If you arrived at the wrong port and got into the wrong hands in Sweden you could have some troubles, because despite being a very progressive country, it's still got right-wing, fascist elements. There's cops in Sweden that wear American flags on their shoulders, even at that time, and they supported Nixon and the war. But Stockholm was pretty well set up. There were U.S. social workers that were on the government payroll to help out. And there was the American Deserters' Committee, which had gained a lot of political allies and was on top of things. So when we arrived we were basically accepted with open arms, and given a stipend to buy a good winter coat, for rent, and language training.

The majority of the guys there were deserters rather than draft resisters. Most of them, frankly, were not strongly motivated by anti-war idealism, although certainly anti-war attitudes were part of the total context that we were in.

On the other hand, a significant minority of us were extremely active—that's where I became politically active and aware. We did a lot of good work, in conjunction with the Swedish anti-war movement. Of course, you have to keep in mind that during the entire war, no more than 800 men came to Sweden, and there were never more than 500 at one time at the height, and they were spread around Sweden, as opposed to Canada, in which there were at least 60,000 men who came up there fleeing the war.

I got the first draft notice in April, 1968, a couple of days after Martin Luther King was killed and the rebellion swept the cities. I was in no mood to show up at the Army. I sent them a notice back and said I'm too busy right now. So then they hand-delivered me a notice saying I should show up in June—the people who delivered it said they were Military Police. After going through testing they sufficiently scared me about the prospect of going to Vietnam that I switched to a three-year enlistment, which I thought would get me out of going to Vietnam. It turned out that wasn't true. I was sent to Fort Bragg, North Carolina. We go by this big sign, "Welcome to KKK Country" outside the base and it was like, *what did they get us into here*? What really introduced me to reading more about Vietnam was a developing black consciousness. Malcolm X wrote quite a bit on Vietnam—what the U.S. was doing there and how ridiculous it was for people to talk about they were for justice, but then go off and help America oppress other people, especially when your people are oppressed at home in America.

I was sent to Germany and about a week after Nixon's speech about the withdrawal from Vietnam they levied half of my unit to Vietnam. Very interesting timing. I came back to the States with orders to Vietnam. I talked with a lot of GIs to try to get the deal on what the war was really about. They would say things like, the My Lai massacre, that was SOP—standard operating procedure.

I've got orders to report for Vietnam on December 31st, and on the 5th I heard that Fred Hampton and Mark Clark were murdered. The Chicago police staked out the house, and at three in the morning, they shoot their way in and blow these guys away. Then I hear the Black Panthers' side of the story and I said, "Wow, the police carried out a search and destroy mission in the middle of Chicago!"

Then they attacked the L.A. Black Panthers' headquarters and there were tanks and mortars set up in the streets of L.A. It's like, this war isn't just something over there, it's here too, and I have to decide what side I'm on. I decided I couldn't be a part of the war in Vietnam, I couldn't go fight for America.

Usually you leave your unit in the morning and you have until midnight to report to your next duty station. So that morning a company commander calls out to the first sergeant, "I want you to go to the weapons room, draw out a .45, keep this man in your sight and if he makes a false move you have my authorization to shoot him." I get my stuff and there's a truck waiting and the commander says, "I'm giving you a direct order to get in the truck." I say, "I don't have to because I got until midnight." And he says, "I'm going to have you over there by ten in the morning and then you're going to be out of my hair." I sat down on my duffel bag and said, "I'm not leaving here." I had heard stories of people being forcibly put on the plane and I figured no sense in going any closer than right here. If they're going to forcibly put me on it, they're going to have to drag me across the base in broad daylight with a lot of people around. I ended up in the stockade that morning.

The trial happened four months later. The military judge made it very clear he was not listening. He says, "You guys can make your arguments for the record, I am not going to consider them, I don't care what you have to say, it seems fairly cut and dry to me." He would lay his head down on the desk, look out the window. He got up at one point and said, "I'm going to the bathroom; it would expedite things if you continued to make your arguments while I was gone." They sent a group of us to Leavenworth, including five people out of the "Fort Lewis 6," the name we got for refusing.

DONALD DUNCAN

Heading up operations of a new, very hush-hush project called Delta—a name that lives to this day—I had to pour over MACV intelligence reports almost daily; both those based on information collected by us and those based on two other similar operations. I was absolutely astounded. It was bullshit. Pure fabrication. Routine fabrication. An example? OK. I think a "typical" mission into Tay Ninh province to check out reported VC movement in and around a Michelin rubber plantation makes the point.

We went in at night and reached the plantation perimeter mid-morning where we found well-prepared trenchworks, complete with mortars, machine guns, ammo—but no people! Feeling as naked as jaybirds, we stood up, took deep breaths, deployed across the opening, stepped across the trenches and proceeded through the rubber trees toward the center of the plantation. Just short of the center we were stopped by the sound of voices. Sgt. Minh and I crept forward and involuntarily stepped back in shock. There was at least a battalion of VC grouped around three individuals, one of whom was talking loudly—a troop "education/orientation" session (we called it TI&E). I radioed to have our VN Airborne troops drop in at three designated sites outside the perimeter, then sat back and waited. The next goddamn thing we knew the whole world exploded on us, and for 12 straight hours the area was under constant air bombardment—with us there! What went wrong? Where were the troops? We had Viet Cong running blindly past us, over us and/or trying to bury themselves next to us in the dark.

Miraculously we survived to get to an LZ the next day and as miraculously our VN chopper again got us out amidst .50 caliber fire; we were back at Ton Son Nut. There we were handed a report—already released to the press—telling how many KIAs there were (in the hundreds). I challenged the report inasmuch as we were the only people on the ground and we didn't have a clue how many had been killed. We were too busy scrambling to get our asses to a pick-up point, and there were too many live bodies in the area to be walking around counting dead ones. What I got in response was a bunch of prop-wash about grids and tons of bombs per grid factored by numbers of people in each grid equals x-number of KIAs. When I pointed out that ten of us moved from one grid to another and were not killed, it was ignored—and no apology for overriding our orders, for not informing us or for "dropping," knowing we were in one of those grids.

From that day I grabbed and analyzed every report I could get my hands on having anything to do with intelligence and policy. It was obvious we had no policy and intelligence was whatever MACV said it was. We had reports of ". . . and four VC water buffalo killed," and Marines shooting at "VC sounds" and reporting KIA. Instead of cleaning up corruption in the country, we became the biggest contributors to it. We supported the worst elements in the country. We had nothing to win. The whole thing was a lie.

I signed on for a second hitch in Vietnam, but I couldn't bring the same enthusiasm to it. Oh, I was being offered things—a direct commission to captain, a Silver Star and Legion of Merit . . . All heady stuff for a career soldier. But the idealism and purpose of my being a "Green Beret" and being in Vietnam was confuted at every turn. The administration and the Generals were deceiving the American people and betraying its troops. After 10 1/2 years in the U.S. Army, in the summer of '65, I quietly put in my papers for discharge. Once back in the land of the Big PX I was determined to get out the word.

DAVE CLINE

In training they gave you basically two things: either you were going over there to help the people of South Vietnam fight against Communist aggression, or you were going over to kill commies. My background made me definitely be against the idea of going over to kill commies, so I sort of latched onto the idea we were there to help people—I wanted to believe we were doing the right thing. When I got to Vietnam it really didn't take me but about one day in-country to realize it wasn't true. As soon as you get there the first thing they tell you is you can't trust any of them, they're gooks, they're not human beings.

On January 20, 1967 we were overrun by NVA and this guy ran off to my hole and started shooting in and I started shooting out and he shot me through the knee and I shot him through the chest and killed him. I laid in the hole all night. When the battle ended in the morning, they pulled me out of the hole, put me on a stretcher and carried me over to this guy I'd shot. He was sitting there dead leaning over against this old tree stump, just sitting there, with his rifle across his lap and a couple of bullet holes through his chest. The sergeant said, "Here's this gook you shot, you did a good job." I looked at the guy; he was about the same age as me and I didn't feel any pride in it at all. They gave me a bronze star for that. This is the only person I can say with any certainty that I shot and it blew my mind.

While I was in the hospital in Japan I found a book which was called *The New Legions* by Donald Duncan. Duncan had served 18 months in 'Nam training ARVNs, and he resigned from the military and basically wrote we're fighting on the wrong side. When I read that book it made a lot of sense to me because that's what I saw. So I made a decision I was going to come back to the United States and start working against the war.

I was sent down to Fort Hood and that's when I really got hooked up with the GI movement. They had a coffeehouse in town called the "Oleo Strut," and a newspaper called the *Fatigue Press*, which I got involved with. The Democratic Convention was scheduled for that summer, '68, so they began having riot control training. They called it "The Garden Plot." We decided to organize a movement against it because there was a lot of opposition to the idea of going to Chicago. A lot of guys had just come back from 'Nam and they said, we fought the Vietnamese, now they want you to fight Americans. A lot of people identified with the demonstrators on different levels.

We put together a meeting on the base. We met on a big ballfield right in the middle of the base and there must have been about 70 or 80 GIs there; black guys, white guys. We got a sticker mass-produced, a black hand and a peace sign. The plan was we were going to distribute them to all the troops that were opposed to being used. If they put us on the streets against the demonstrators, we were going to put these stickers on our helmets as a visible sign of solidarity with the demonstrators in opposition to what we were doing. About three days after that almost everyone that was at the meeting got taken off The Garden Plot roster for being subversive. They told the troops if anyone was caught with a sticker they would be court-martialed.

SKIP DELANO

I joined the Army in February 1967. I got to Vietnam in May, and by August I was very clearly against the war and against the military as well. I think for most soldiers, going to Vietnam and seeing the reality of the war, all this mickey mouse bullshit as the whole army was, to actually be in the middle of a war where hundreds of people were being killed everyday, it was just incomprehensible to most of us. I think most of us just immediately opposed that and maybe our understanding of why we opposed it wasn't as sharp as it might have been, but just on a gut level. Having been raised like myself, a Presbyterian, and being active in the church in the area I grew up in, it just wasn't right what was going on in Vietnam. While I was in Vietnam I didn't see any way to take action against the war, so my own response was basically to withdraw from any kind of overt activity that promoted the war.

I came back very committed to fighting this whole machine that sent us there and kept us in Vietnam. I came back with six others who got assigned to Fort McClellan, Alabama—this is where I had taken my training to be a chemical repairman before going to Vietnam. We decided we wanted to try to take some action against the war and decided to put out a paper. I started going up to Atlanta where there was very vibrant youth culture on the streets and an underground newspaper called *A Great Speckled Bird.* I got in touch with some people there who turned me on to somebody who could print the paper for us, and met a guy, another GI who had some experience writing and working on a college paper.

Somehow it all just came together and we started putting out a paper, which we called *Left Face* because I guess, though we were all pretty inexperienced with politics, it was real clear that our views were always to the left and that's where we were looking to—the

Left. We'd have to spend a fair amount of time figuring out how to get the paper out, into hands of people on the base. You'd sneak around at night and you'd run in barracks and you'd throw it on the beds and you'd split and get the hell out of there. I can remember running out and jumping into the trunk of a car and laying in the trunk; the MPs would come and you would be hiding in the trunk of some cars and hoping you wouldn't get caught. Because if you got caught, you could get six months in the stockade, the potential punishment for distributing unauthorized literature, which the papers were characterized as.

Immediately after we put out the first paper, in late October of '69, about 30 of us on the base signed a petition being circulated by the GI Press Service in support of a demonstration coming up on November 15th in Washington. As soon as it appeared in *The New York Times,* it was sort of like all hell broke loose on that base because people's names were on that ad. Everybody who signed it got called in by Military Intelligence and interrogated and harangued and people lost their security clearances and things like that. I thought and believed very much that since I had been in Vietnam, I had every right to comment on it to other people. In fact, I had a responsibility, and I took it seriously. I thought it was my democratic right to speak out and I was really shocked to find out that wasn't reality or freedom in America.

TERRY IRVIN

G I Alliance and the GIs, Sailors and Airmen's Coalition had joined forces at Fort Lewis and McChord Air Base in Washington. In 1971 we decided a fun thing to do for the 4th of July would be to pass out copies of the Declaration of Independence on base. Somebody found a copy of the Declaration of Independence and said, "Have you ever read this thing? This is really great stuff." And so we underlined things we wanted highlighted: certain unalienable rights, among these life, liberty and the pursuit of happiness . . . and whenever any form of government becomes destructive to these ends it is the right of the people to alter or abolish it and institute a new government . . . and it is their right, it is their duty to throw off such government and provide new guards for their future security . . . and he has erected a multitude of new offices, sent swarms of officers to harass our people and eke out their substance, is combined with others to subject us to jurisdiction foreign to our constitution, imposing taxes without our consent, depriving us in many cases of benefits by trial of jury—which was a big complaint of ours. Military justice is almost as big an oxymoron as "military intelligence."

We went to the main PX on pay day when everybody would be there. There were probably a dozen GIs and three or four civilians. Word got out within 20 minutes and the MPs show up, swarms of them all over us. I was hauled off with my friend Henry Valenti and somehow we ended up having these leaflets with us. We were throwing them out of the window of the cop car as they hauled us off singing America the Beautiful.

We were charged with distributing unauthorized literature on base. It hadn't been approved by the brass. We had tried and tried to get approval to distribute the *Lewis-McChord Free Press* on base

and could not do it. Hell, they had skin magazines that were ten times more offensive than anything we put out, and they were everywhere. So why couldn't we put out our newspaper on base? I was the only guy who didn't take an Article 15, I decided I was going to fight this. I said I wanted to waive trial and elected to go to a general court-martial.

Now, in the meantime, the press is having a field day with this. We got on Walter Cronkite, we were his closing story on the CBS Evening News, this group of GIs that was arrested for passing out the Declaration of Independence on the 4th of July at Fort Lewis. And the brass's response to this was that all the charges had been dropped and "just pay no attention to these people, we're not going to press charges." Yet I'm still up for general court-martial, facing three years in Leavenworth.

Finally, I went to see my lawyer and he said, "Something very interesting has happened. They can't come up with any witnesses that said they saw you passing these things out. They have no proof against you." Now, like I said, we had these pamphlets with us in the police cars, in the jail cells, we're shoving them through the bars of the jail cell, passing them out to the MPs there in the Provost Marshall's Office. But they couldn't come up with a witness who said they'd seen me doing this? . . . So they dropped the charges.

TOM: Curt and I had only known each other for one day in Vietnam and less than a day at Fort Carson in Colorado Springs when we decided to start a newspaper.

CURT: I was sent to the Fort Carson Army Hospital closed circuit radio station that Tom had been assigned to and basically given the job that he had once had, which was a staff announcer. Someone commented that there was someone else in the unit from the 10th PsyOp Battalion, and he told me who it was, and I remembered Tom because the day we met we had undertaken a sort of adventure together. But I remembered we had a lot in common—we'd gone through DINFOS (Defense Information School) together; he had a journalism background and I had a radio background, we both ended up in PsyOps and we were both sour-graping. The communication there was pretty amazing.

I had some copies of a battalion newspaper from Vietnam called *Dimension*, which it turns out Tom had started before I got there and that I had become editor of. So he was looking through those magazines and seeing the people he had been in Vietnam with and what had happened to them. It was like a continuation of what happened after he left. And in the course of talking about the war and our experiences and what are we doing here and what are we going to do about it, we thought let's start a newspaper because there isn't one here.

TOM: I think we were catalysts on each other.

CURT: I was intent upon showing up at Fort Carson and saying I quit . . .

TOM: Or being a conscientious objector . . .

CURT: Or making some kind of a major stink. I was pretty pissed about the whole thing and fresh off the boat. I was ready to go in there and do something very radical. I hadn't really quite figured out what yet.

TOM: And I said, "Well Curt, if you're going to become a CO, it's really pretty meaningless. We should do something else. We're at a hospital; once a year they maybe make us go out to the rifle range and fire a couple of shots, but otherwise we're hardly even really in the Army." I'm not sure who came up with the idea of actually doing a newspaper first, but it came up and once it came up I think we just hopped on that idea. We said, "Yeah, that's it, a newspaper. We know how to do it, we've done it."

CURT: So we immediately got into it. It was August 9th we got the first issue out. The name just came to me, "*aboveground*." Someone was saying, "Hey you're going to do an underground newspaper." And I said, "No, we're going to be totally above ground." That's how the name came about. The first issue we were not sure what level of commitment we wanted to get into, so the actual first issue we didn't even put our names in. We called ourselves "this reporter" and "that reporter." And then after we came out with that first issue, they figured out who we were pretty much straight away.

TOM: Within two days I think after we distributed it, they had us on the carpet. Military Intelligence. They summarily transferred us. We had been roommates and it was real easy for us to bat around ideas and put out the newspaper. In fact, we even had a little darkroom in our room.

CURT: We were industrious little investigative reporters; wrote some really good stories actually while we were there. We caught this general who was the commander of the post flying helicopters without a pilot's license. When we were ready to run that one they sent the FBI around to see our printer down in Colorado Springs and basically threatened to shut him down. The printer wouldn't print it.

TOM: They called us and he said we're not going to print the paper. I said, why not? And he goes, "Well, the Army came in here and the FBI and they wanted proofs and this 'n that and they wanted to see the thing and it was just too much of a hassle and we're just not going to do it." But there was a lot of press coverage about that incident and an editor and publisher of this paper in Littleton, Colorado, offered to print the newspaper for us. He said, "I disagree with what you guys are saying about the war, but I believe absolutely in your right to say it without interference from the FBI or from Military Intelligence. You have the First Amendment right to say that and I very much support that."

Within I think about a month of us coming out with the first issue, in fact I think it may have even been the day before the second issue came out, they split us up. They transferred both of us out of the United States Army Hospital at Fort Carson, and they sent Curt up to Fitzsimmons Army Hospital in Denver 70 miles away, and they sent me over to a line artillery unit. We had almost a whole month to get out the next issue, but the process became a lot harder for Curt and I to coordinate. We got together a lot less frequently.

CURT: Yeah, there was a lot of driving.

TOM: And money became a concern. But for the third issue a woman that I ran into kept us going. Her husband had just been killed in Vietnam through friendly fire, and she donated enough money for one issue from the GI life insurance policy that she got. And the United States Servicemen's Fund was the single biggest contributor.

CURT: We did stuff in the paper with curfews and issues that affected soldiers. And we found out about this plan for military interdiction in civilian activities, like big demonstrations and Kent State. It was code named "Garden Plot" and it had to do with Fort Carson soldiers being in a position of readiness to be dispatched anywhere.

TOM: That one we did run in *aboveground*, and at least a year later it made front page news. We scooped it by a year. Another story we never printed was after the first issue came out. A crazy sergeant I was working with up at the registrar section, a former Green Beret, was working at K-Mart at night in the sporting goods department just taking orders. What do you need? Well, come out by the back door and I'll sell it to you for 20 bucks. You want that rifle? That costs $79.95, and I'll sell it to you for 20 bucks or whatever. And he was just ripping it off from K-Mart and making 20 bucks. So anyhow he said, "Hey this is pretty cool this paper that you have. You want a story?" He goes, "You know that Gulf of Tonkin thing? I was in a Green Beret sapper team and we were sent up to blow up, with satchel charges and shit like that, and infiltrate and do sapper attacks on those PT bases there. We were there to provoke those PT bases, those PT boats. And we'd blow up other things in the vicinity so that those PT boats would go out and shoot up those destroyers, or at least fire some shots at those destroyers." He was just such a wild bullshitter, freelance, seat-of-the-pants kind of a guy, I thought, oh yeah right. And of course later on that all came out in the Pentagon papers—and this is in August of 1969 that this guy said you ought to interview me.

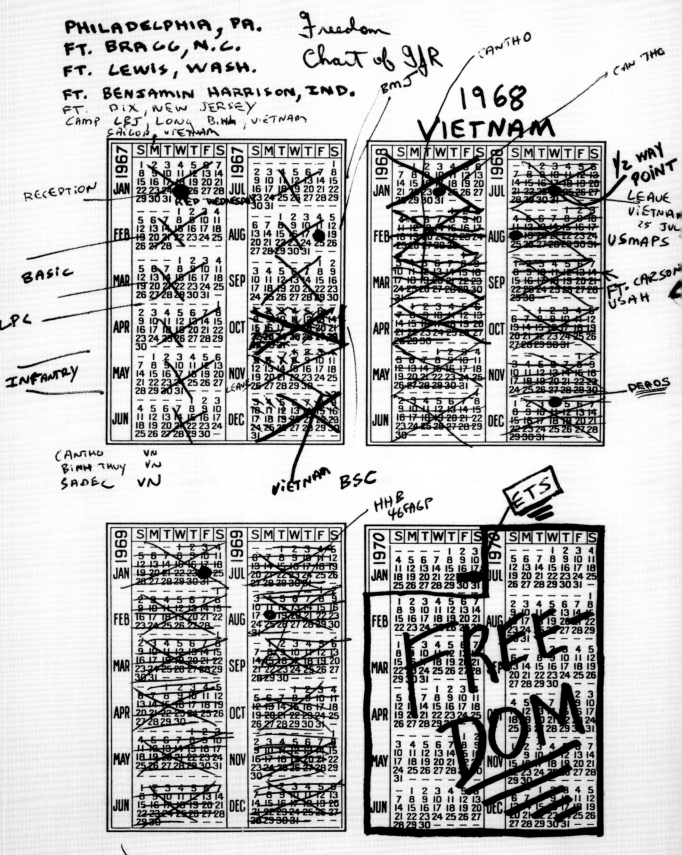

PHILADELPHIA, PA.
FT. BRAGG, N.C.
FT. LEWIS, WASH.
FT. BENJAMIN HARRISON, IND.
FT. DIX, NEW JERSEY
CAMP LBJ, LONG BINH, VIETNAM
SAIGON, VIETNAM

Freedom
Chart of JJR

1968
VIETNAM

BMJ
CANTHO
CAN THO

RECEPTION
BASIC
LPC
INFANTRY

½ WAY POINT
LEAVE VIETNAM
25 JUL
USMAPS
FT. CARSON
USAH
DEROS

CANTHO   VN
BINH THUY   VN
SADEC   VN

VIETNAM   BSC

HHB
46 FAGP

ETS

FREEDOM

CAN THO, RVN
SADEC, RVN
VINH LONG, RVN

46TH FAGP

OLIVER HIRSCH

After going back and forth for months about what was going on in Vietnam, and arguing about what to do about the whole thing, a friend and I decided one day that that was it: we were not going. Confronting the military outright wasn't my first thought about how to go about staying out of the war, so I cooked up a story and told my CO that the level of violence I was surrounded by in the military had gotten me to the point where I could commit an act of violence to anyone (and the implication included him) without any compunction. I knew they were going to try and talk me out of it, so I wanted to have one thing to say, and I said it over and over again. As I had hoped, I ended up at the nut ward at the Presidio. And when the four-inch door slammed shut behind me, I figured, I've done something that has changed my future—there's *no* turning back.

After a few weeks, my Marine psychiatrist told me I was going back to active duty. So the next morning I conned a guard into letting me go outside where a friend from the locked ward upstairs threw me my shoes. In a minute I was off the base in my pajamas—this was San Francisco in 1968, and nobody gave me a second look. I went directly to the War Resisters League in Haight-Ashbury; they farmed me out to a hippie commune where I could take time to figure out what the hell I was going to do. After a few weeks, a friend came by to tell me there were eight AWOL GIs who had taken sanctuary in a church in Haight-Ashbury, and that they were going to make as big a stink as they could. Along with the eight soldiers, there were many people from the religious and resistance community who wanted to stand with the GIs. The plan that emerged was for members of the support community to chain themselves to the AWOL soldiers who were publicly resigning from the military. I asked if they were encouraging other GIs to join. They said, "sure!" And that was it: we were the "Nine for Peace."

I recall it as a very busy and intense time. The press came immediately, and in large numbers, and we were international news overnight. The reaction of the military and the powers-that-be was pretty humorous, and we loved every minute of it. What we did really blindsided them. There were no illusions about whether or not we were going to jail; but I think there was a real spirit of "whatever it took."

There were various services and programs, and planning sessions amongst the nine of us to hammer out what our stand was going to be. On the second day a stewardess came to the church and told us she had overheard a couple of her passengers talking about blowing the protest away. It was decided that the entire sanctuary was to be moved to a church in Marin City.

The next morning—three days after the sanctuary began—we were busted. I remember seeing the lines of police cars and vans as they gathered at the off-ramp off Highway 101, sort of in a military formation. Then they all pulled out and around to the front of the church. When they came in they had to break up a full-fledged church communion service as the cameras rolled. They waded into the crowd and grimly cut our chains and handcuffed us.

I was taken to the stockade at Hamilton Air Force Base and given a brochure by the sergeant in charge that gave me my choices for the kind of training I wanted when I got to Leavenworth—there was no question but that I was going to Leavenworth. So I was floored when they came up to me in the prison yard and told me they had accepted my resignation "for the good of the service," and that they were going to throw me out, rather than go ahead with my court-martial. Within hours I went from facing years in prison, like my fellow Nine for Peace brothers, to standing on the side of the highway in civilian clothes—free as a man can be in this country.

PROTEST AGAINST WAR — Eight servicemen including Keith Mather of San Bruno, third from left in rear row, have chained themselves to clergymen at the Howard Presbyterian Church in San Francisco as a protest to the war in Vietnam, second from left is the Rev. Andrew Juvenall, formerly from San Bruno now with the Hamilton Methodist Church in San Francisco. (AP Wirephoto)

Anti-War 'Chain Gang' Goes to Churc

9 AWOL GIs Out of Hiding

By DEXTER WAUGH

The small car screeched to a step in front of Howard Presbyterian Church at Oak and Baker Streets and three AWOL servicemen, chained with three clergymen, piled out.

An announcement by the church proclaimed 1 p.m. yesterday as the beginning of a 48-hour worship service "of communion and celebration to acknowledge the declaration of freedom of these young men present who have left the military service for reasons of conscience."

The three men, recently emerged from the underground of hiding, stood in the warm sun, linked in pairs to their clergymen. Presently they were joined by six more AWOLs, each chained to a clergyman. A lady's gawking face hung out of the window of a passing car. The 18 men filed inside the church.

RELIEF

Keith Mather, 21, of San Bruno, admitted to a certain "relief" by coming out in the open. He has been absent without official leave from Fort Lewis, Washington, since March 20. He was joined at the wrist by a simple chain and padlock to the Rev. George P. Carter, pastor of the Methodist Church in Mill Valley.

"The chains between clergy and young men symbolize the bonds of solidarity and brotherhood between all men," said the Rev. Tom Dietrich, pastor of the Howard Presbyterian Church.

Father Joseph R. Sonntag, a Franciscan priest to whom Robinson was chained, said he joined the demonstration "mainly to show the support

of the church. I feel it is an act of conscience on their part, and I agree with their views on the war."

PRIEST AGREES

All of the nine said they left the service for reasons of conscience. John Robinson, an 18-year-old Marine from Westport, Conn., said his enlistment was "impulsive," that his "ideas about war hadn't solidified" until he left.

chino High School in San Bruno, said he left the service because "I am opposed to the war and I don't believe in killing my fellow man. I was forced by being drafted to compromise my ideals."

He added that "I was being recycled into a company bound for Vietnam, and I knew I couldn't fight." He had talked to his parents, and "they are behind me."

STANDS BY

The Rev. Mr. Carter, who for a while seemed bound to following Mather around, indicated his conscience compelled him to "stand by him." He didn't intend it as a joke. The 31-year-old Rev. Mr. Carter seemed unconcerned about his Mill Valley parish — "they are good, honest people; but some won't like it (his action)."

Mather and the eight other AWOL servicemen thought it highly likely that their participation in the 48 hour session would attract the military police and F.B.I. from which they have been hiding. Mather, at least, was resigned to capture. "I've been expecting it all along, anyway."

Paul Howard, of R.F.I. Lisa, and Dale Herrin of Garland, Tex., were stationed at Treasure Island together when they decided to leave.

Howard said he didn't try the more official route of applying for conscientious objector status because "not enough people would know what I'm doing, and why." He preferred, instead, this "public confrontation."

Howard, 21, has been AWOL since July 5. Herrin, who met Howard in February, left at the same time, even though he was in electronics school and didn't figure he had "much chance of going to Vietnam."

Others included James Seymour, of Deer Park, N.Y., Steve Anderson, of Las Vegas, Nevada, Chuck Jones, of Fernandina Beach, Fla., and George Danis, of Atlanta, Ga., all absent from the Army, and Oliver Hirsch.

"AN ACT OF CONSCIENCE"
John Robinson chained to Father Joseph Sonntag
—Examiner Photo

from the Air Force.

Other clergymen participating are the Rev. Andrew Juvinall, pastor of Hamilton Methodist Church of San Francisco; Father Mark W. Sullivan, Roman Catholic Diocese of Rochester, N.Y.;

the Rev. Charles G. Robertson Jr., United Presbyterian minister and campus pastor for the Marin County Council of Churches at the College of Marin; Father Richard York, Episcopalian priest with the Free Church in Berkeley; the

At Howard Presbyterian Church . . .

Rev. Phil Farnham, United Church of Christ; and Ji Anderson, seminarian Francisco Theological Se nary.

The Rev. M. Dietrich representatives of vario churches and groups in

---

Bruno Youth Protests War

(Continued From Page 1)

drafted six months ago and sent at Fort Lewis, Wash., for basic combat training.

He has been AWOL (absent without leave) for the past four months, according to his mother.

Mather and seven other young servicemen, each chained to a clergyman, entered Howard Presbyterian Church in San Francisco Sunday to participate in what one of the ministers termed a "tearful celebration" of young men who refuse to go to war.

The reference, according to the Rev. Tom Dietrich, pastor at Howard Presbyterian, is to a passage from the Old Testament Book of Jeremiah.

"The Book of Jeremiah tearfully celebrates young men who refuse to serve, just as it celebrates those who serve," the Rev. Mr. Dietrich said.

Mather was working and attending night school when he received his draft call earlier this year, Mrs. Mather said, and had planned to attend College of San Mateo.

He has been considering the best way to make known his feelings on the war, and this was his decision. He told me recently he wished he had never gone into the service at all, and had made his stand at the time he was inducted.

Mather and the other young men participating in the San Francisco protest have stated they "came to their senses" about the war after serving in the military for a brief period.

Brunan To Hard Labor For 4 Years

SAN FRANCISCO (AP) — Pvt. Keith A Mather, 21, of San Bruno, one of nine servicemen who chained themselves to clergymen July 16 and announced they were "dropout" of the Vietnam war was convicted Tuesday by a court martial of desertion and willful disobedience of an order.

He was given a dishonorable discharge and sentenced to four years at hard labor.

Eight of the nine AWOL servicemen have been before courtmartial and all have been convicted. A Marine was sentenced to six months, a sailor got three years, an airman was discharged but not sentenced, and the sentence for five soldiers ranged from two to four years.

After Mather's conviction, two women sprayed a room at the Presidio of San Francisco with red paint and were arrested.

...NAN AWOL
...r Says
...nt To
Protest War

The mother of one of eight young servicemen protesting the Vietnamese War in a "tearful celebration" in San Francisco today said her son is "very sincere, and prepared to face whatever comes" from his stand.

Mrs. Lee Mather, 249 San Marco, San Bruno, said her son, Keith Mather, 21, is "only expressing the views which he has been taught at home.

"I have always been against killing, and I have taught my children to believe the same way," Mrs. Mather, the daughter of a Baptist minister, said in an interview today.

She said that Keith, oldest of her three boys, "has never killed anything in his life, hates guns, and didn't want to go into the Army in the first place."

A former Capuchino High School student, Mather was

(Please See Page 10, Column)

War 'Chain Gang'
Bomb Threat Disrupts Protest

A bomb threat forced the evacuation last night of the unusual chain-link war protest at Howard Presbyterian Church in the Haight-Ashbury.

Nine servicemen who say they've "resigned" from the military — and each shackled to the wrist of a clergyman — were hurriedly transferred to St. Andrew's United Presbyterian Church in Marin City.

The Rev. Tom Dieterich, pastor of the Haight-Ashbury church at Oak and Baker streets, said his secretary, Norma Ritzke, received a call about 6:30 p.m. from a woman who refused to identify herself.

The woman said she had overheard two men at the Greyhound bus station saying that they were going to take a bomb out to the church and separate the protesting servicemen and clergymen, Mrs. Ritzke said.

The church was cleared, and police and church leaders searched it, but found no explosive. Nevertheless, the police advised the elders not to use the church during the night, and they agreed.

One more serviceman

joined the ranks of the protestors yesterday.

The latest addition — there were eight Monday morning — is Oliver Hirsch, 21, a personable young man who said he came in out of the cold to protest war and lend his support to his eight comrades who walked away from their posts.

The demonstration, billed as a "tearful celebration" against the war in Vietnam, started at 1 p.m. Monday and is scheduled to end around 10 a.m. today.

The protesters said they were "acting out of Christian motives." Federal and military law enforcement agencies weren't acting at all.

"No, we haven't washed our hands of the matter," a military spokesman said somewhat peevishly, listening to a radio talkshow's interview of the nine servicemen.

But he declined to say if the protesters — and some are listed as deserters — would be arrested.

Hirsch, an Air Force sergeant, said he walked away from his post six weeks ago and promptly came down to help out when he heard what his comrades were doing.

Marine Protester's Jail Term

Portsmouth, N.H.

Marine Private John Robinson, 19, of Sarasota, Fla., due to be let out of the Portsmouth Naval Prison yesterday, will not be released until he regains his health impaired by a hunger strike, officials said.

Robinson, who began a hunger strike October 27 to protest the Vietnam war, served the last day of a six-month sentence yesterday.

He was sentenced for being AWOL last summer and taking part in a protest with eight other servicemen in San Francisco.

Robinson originally was sentenced to a bad conduct discharge, but that has since been lifted.

He is scheduled to return to active duty once he regains some weight and gets over a kidney infection contracted during the hunger strike, which caused his weight to drop from 200 pounds to 140 pounds.

Authorities shifted Robinson from the prison to the base hospital for his health's sake, and force-fed him for a time, officials said. It was reported yesterday that Robinson is taking food

Page 2— The ADVANCE-STAR, Burlingame, California   Friday, July 19

What Fate for 9

By GEORGE NEWMAN

A legal team was chosen yesterday to defend the nine AWOL servicemen whose 48-hour Vietnam War protest ended Wednesday with their arrest outside a Marin City church.

Included among those taken into custody by Armed Forces Police was 21-year-old Keith Mather of San Bruno, a Capuchino High School graduate, who told reporters he was responding to the protest movement as "an act of conscience."

Engelskirchen said he could not indicate what action he would take on the youth's behalf until formal charges were filed. Meanwhile, an Army spokesman at the Presidio in San Francisco told The Advance-

20, while undergoing advanced training for infantry duty in Vietnam. He was drafted last September.

"Attorney Howard Engelskirchen of San Francisco said he had been asked by officials backing the protest to represent Mather. Each of the other eight are being assigned individual counsel.

Those involved could be charged with being absent without leave, an offense which normally carries less severe penalties. Or they could face a more serious charge of military desertion, which carries a penalty of from six months to

Star that Mather was bein in the stockade there alon several of the other youths.

An investigation would be conducted and each case individually studied before a sion could be made with r to charges, the spokesman s

Those involved could charged with being absent out leave, an offense which normally carries less severe penalties. Or they could face more serious charge of mil desertion, which carries a p ty of from six months to years' imprisonment.

Last T. I.
In 'Chain

The last of the nine servicemen who chained themselves to clergymen here last July was sentenced to two years' hard labor by a Navy court-martial at Treasure Island yesterday.

Seaman Paul Diane Howard, 22, of Roy, Utah, was found guilty of unauthorized absence — reduced from the more serious charge of desertion — and of disobeying an order to put on his uniform in the Treasure Island brig.

Howard will also forfeit his pay and allowances and was reduced to the lowest enlisted grade.

Howard and eight other servicemen sang peace songs at Howard Presbyterian Church here. After a bomb threat, they moved to a Marin City church, where military police arrested them July 17 and cut the chains binding them to the Bay Area clergymen.

Another seaman, Dale E. Herrin, 20, of Garland, Tex., tex...

nked to Father Richard York
—Examiner photo by George Place

be "sleeping ... night and two formal ... were sched- ... p.m. both ... Baer was ... how the

eight men, who hadn't known each other very long, had gotten together, nor was any sponsor named. The War Resistors League, which counsels young men in refusing to serve, was named as one of the supporters of the service.

r Foes?

...uths were being ... ckade, some 30 ... ouped outside at ... street gate Wed- ... began a vigil in

... me, some 50 Pe- ... turned out for ... ing at the First ... ch of Burlin- ... the AWOL serv- ... ve appeared. ... the audience ... three of the ... ed in the pro- ... arles G. Rob- ... byterian min- ... c of Marin; the

Rev. Mark W. Sullivan, Roman Catholic priest of Rochester, N.Y.; and the Rev. George P. Carter, pastor of the Methodist Church of Mill Valley.

The Rev. Mr. Carter had served as pastor of the Crystal Springs Methodist Church in San Mateo until last year.

Another clergyman taking part in the protest was the Rev. Andrew Juvinall, pastor of the Hamilton Methodist Church of San Francisco. The Reverend Mr. Juvinall had formerly served with the Community Methodist Church in San Bruno.

The program at the Burlingame church went off without incident, it was reported.

Asked to comment on her son's arrest, Mrs. Lee Mather, of 249 San Marco Ave., San Bruno, said she was relieved.

"It was something they had expected any moment," she said.

The youth's mother explained that Keith was prepared to accept whatever consequences might be in store for him.

Declaring herself to be in sympathy with her son's position, Mrs. Mather said:

"The youth of today are sick and tired of the hypocrisy in our society.

"The way they are taught to kill selectively . . . they simply will not go along with it anymore!"

The nine AWOL servicemen were arrested Wednesday as they prepared to accept Holy Communion at St. Andrew's Presbyterian Church in Marin City.

Each chained to the wrist of a clergyman, the demonstrators were forced to move to the church late Tuesday from the Howard Presbyterian Church in San Francisco after authorities received a bomb threat call there.

Military police allowed the youths to receive their Communion — bread and wine — before they voluntarily marched outside.

There, the padlocked chains were snipped with a pair of heavy bolt cutters and the youths were hustled off in two waiting paddy wagons.

The clergymen were not arrested.

A military policeman snapped the chains on one of the anti-war protesters outside St. Andrews Church.

To Stockade
MP's Break Up GI 'Chain Gang'

Military police ended the "Chain gang" anti-war protest of AWOLs and clergymen at a Marin City church today amid emotional outbursts of supporters, many of them weeping women.

When the protesters' Community Service of Liberation" was over, the MPs, who had watched quietly, marched the servicemen and clergymen, chained together in pairs, out of the edifice to a waiting paddy wagon.

There the MPs, using big bolt cutters, cut the chains and put the soldiers into the wagon for their trip to the Presidio's stockade.

Nine servicemen and nine clergymen were the principals in the scene. They began their protest Monday at Howard Presbyterian Church, Oak and Baker Streets, San Francisco.

ALLOW PROTEST

MPs in five cars dropped by but did not interfere, allowing the protest to run its full 48 hours before they acted. The demonstration was moved to the St. Andrew Presbyterian Church in Marin City after a woman reported she had overheard a threat to bomb the San Francisco church.

The chained pairs arrived at the Marin church in private cars at 9:30 p.m. yesterday. They spent the night there. About 9 a.m. they formed a circle and, amid chants, resumed the service.

The MPs entered a little after 10. Rev. James Symons, co-minister of the church, in effect invited them to join the "communion."

"This is Christ's table," he said, "and all here are invited to share in this communion."

WATCH WINE

The MPs watched while wine was poured from a silver chalice and bread was broken. Then they quietly but firmly went into action. Standing by at a sheriff's substation down the street was Sheriff Louis Mountanus with a number of deputies, but there was no need for them.

As the AWOLs were marched out they held their arms high, fingers making the V-sign.

John Robinson, 18, a Marine from Westport, Conn., told newsmen as the chains binding him to a clergyman were cut —

"Cutting of these chains does not really break the bonds. I hope what we're doing will give some kind of enlightenment to others."

REV. PRESIDENT

Brian Drolet, a San Francisco AWOL and a spokesman for the group, said most of them had gone "over the hill" while in San Francisco and had met by accident at the Howard Church. It was here, he said, that the plan for the chain gang protest was developed.

He estimated, through contacts with various anti-war organizations, that there are 100 or more AWOLs in the Bay Area at this time.

r. 5, 1969

... ce ... st

... enced to ... abor and a ... harge for ... isobedience

... martials. ... ates were ... ears' hard ... rable dis- ... got two ... rable dis- ... sentences ... d on ap-

... was given ... arge and ... bor, later ... ouths. A ... requested ... harge in- ... rtial. ... martial, ... tober, ... ly for a ... tion, aft- ... R. Jay ... Howard ... at the ... dents in

... st testi- ... sane at ... ng pro- ... stion.

...mother, Mrs. Lee Mather... said she went to Jones' ... soldier's own mother was in ...

"I don't know what the m... see where these boys h... but the military feels they b...

Mrs. Mather said she d... fense her son and his civil ... leskirchen, San Francisco, ... attorney will just have to g...

In addition to Engleski... fended by an officer from t... al's office. The court marti... of eight Army men, a thir... Mather so desires.

The soldier's mother say... son every Sunday for a ... finement.

"He says the treatment is not always good at the stockade, but they don't complain too much," Mrs. Mather said. "His biggest complaint is the harassment that goes with the military," Mrs. Mather said.

KEITH MATHER

My mother gave me an address and phone number of the War Resisters League. I met up with these people and they introduced me to other AWOL GIs. A connection, finally! All these people with short hair, all AWOL, all doing the same thing—resisting the war. People at WRL suggested the idea of taking sanctuary in a church. Out of that idea came chains connecting our arms with those of priests and ministers. This represented the bonds between man, and between the clergy and these AWOL servicemen. We became known as the "Nine for Peace." At the close of the service, we were arrested by the Military Police.

All the Army guys were sent to Presidio. They paraded NCOs by to look at us—"Oh, these are those peace freaks" and "We're going to send you off to Vietnam anyway, we're going to take you out and put you on an airplane tonight." That scared us. I heard somebody talking about this guy sitting there in his cell in his underwear, refusing to wear his uniform. I'm going, all right, there's people here resisting. We started to network.

Richard Bunch was a disturbed kid who had been to Vietnam and was in prison on an AWOL charge. The guards would withhold his psychiatric medication. I didn't know him well, but I spoke to him briefly several times and then the next thing I knew he was murdered by a prison guard. It scared the shit out of us all. We were all nervous, itching to get out, and itching to figure out what happened. There was a miniature riot, people were going, "it ain't worth it anymore, they're killing us."

Then they had a memorial service. We all went because he meant something to us. He was one of us, not one of them. The chaplain stated it was justifiable homicide. We started throwing chairs in every direction and yelling. We knew then that the chain of command was trying to cover up the murder. We realized we had to do something. We decided to do something at roll call after chow. A name was called, a couple people shuffled, so I took a step and I brushed a guy aside. I heard steps behind me so I kept walking. We got over to the lawn; I turned and half the formation was coming toward me. We all locked arms and sat down. From that time on we were known as the "Presidio 27." Walter Pawlowski stood up and read the list of grievances. The captain ordered us to get up and then opened the book and started reading us the mutiny act. About that time, about 60 MPs arrived. They got us inside. Walter and I were thrown into solitary confinement and named as the ringleaders right off the bat. We felt we could do a lot of damage if we took away their two star defendants, so after solitary we started planning our escape. Christmas Eve day 1968, we bailed out of a window while we were putting our work tools away and jogged off the post.

On New Year's Eve we went to Canada. I lived there until 1980 when I came back to live with my two children. In 1984 I was going along like there was nothing wrong. I got a call that someone had found my driver's license. When I went to the police station to get it, they arrested me on my old warrant. They took me to the Presidio, then to the stockade at Fort Ord, and then to Fort Riley, Kansas. I was 38, in prison with 20-year-olds. While I was imprisoned former Presidio 27 and others campaigned to get me released. After serving four months I was released from the military in April 1985. My dishonorable discharge states I had been in the military for 17 years and 2 months.

RANDY ROWLAND

October 12, 1968 was going to be the first big GI and Veterans' March for Peace in the San Francisco Bay area. And so, like the "Nine for Peace," some of us who were AWOL were going to turn ourselves in, in conjunction with the march. On the 11th there was an article in the paper that said a prisoner at the Presidio stockade had been shotgunned and killed. Nobody on the outside knew what was going on, so my assignment was to go into the stockade, find out what's going on and get the message out.

The first thing I did is try and find Keith Mather. I found out that they had in fact shotgunned this guy Richard Bunch. Keith and I and Walter Pawlowski and a few others said we got to do something. You're talking about some tough, quality people here. I think I was the only guy that had graduated from high school. They were working class and it was the very thing that made the GI movement in that period unusual and really dangerous I think to the establishment; that these weren't the educated kids, these weren't the kids sitting around intellectually singing hootenanny songs. These were guys who were disenfranchised and oppressed and they were taking it up. That's what made the GI movement such a threat.

Saturday night we had a meeting in the cellblock, which was then taken to other cellblocks. We were going to sit down, refuse to get up and we were going to sing. The black GIs decided they weren't going to do it because they figured they were the only ones who'd get punished. It wasn't clear who else was going to do it and who wasn't . . . I guess it never occurred to me that I wouldn't do it. Every morning they had a formation and did roll call, because as prisoners they count you all the time. So on roll call formation, some of us broke ranks and walked over there. The brass started freaking out instantly. We sat down, linked arms and started singing. The

main song was "We Shall Overcome." In the very act of breaking ranks and going to do it we said, *fuck it*, we don't care what happens, we're just going to do it. It was an elation, like an energy, people were up. We didn't give a shit what they did. The commandant came over and tried to read the mutiny article to us. We just sang louder whenever he tried to talk. We were not going to be intimidated, even though it's a capital offense.

We had agreed that one person was going to stand up and read our demands, and that person was Walter Pawlowski, who was very popular among the guys. He read the list of our demands, and asked for a response. It was all polite . . . "May I have your response sir?" And of course they didn't have any response. So we just kept singing and pretty soon up comes the fire truck. The firemen get out and they're standing around. We didn't know it at the time, but later we found out they told the firemen to squirt us, and the firemen said no, we fight fires, we don't do this shit. All we knew is the fire trucks were there, but we didn't get squirted. The camera guys were running around taking pictures for evidence, but instead of trying to hide we'd grin for them.

Then they brought in this company of MPs, with their riot stuff on, their gas masks and their big sticks. We just kept singing. Pretty soon the MPs came over and started grabbing people. They stuck us all together in one cellblock, which was great and made it easier to build unity, and charged us with mutiny. The Presidio 27 became an organized force then, we bonded together in a big way. We were steadfast, we never wavered. Never once did anybody apologize or say I wish I hadn't done it.

ROGER BROOMFIELD

I was drafted at 19 years old. My friend and I picked MP school—we thought of Market Street in San Francisco, wearing our MP dress uniforms and walking down the street, talking to the girls and all. Not knowing that most all MPs went to Vietnam and had a high casualty rate. After serving some time in Germany, the Army assigned me to the Presidio stockade as a guard. Within weeks I became the senior guard. I had absolutely no training to be a stockade guard. I was trained to be a street policeman, to do traffic primarily. We started out with 40 or 43 prisoners at the Presidio and quite rapidly it was up to 130. These guys were there for being AWOL and refusing to go to Vietnam. And they were just people, just like me, except that I didn't refuse to go to Vietnam because I didn't have to make that choice. If I had had to, I think they would have put me in the stockade—full time instead of as a guard. The place was extremely overcrowded and we spilled over into another barracks next door. The conditions were atrocious.

So they bring in this prisoner, Richard Bunch, and he was like a deer; flighty, nervous tension bound up. He must have been 19, but he seemed like a 12- or 14-year-old kid. This guy's in bad shape. Probably within a week of the time he came in—it was one of my days off—they had him out on work detail and he started to run. It was the guard's orders if somebody runs to shoot him. And they shot this guy with a 12-gauge shotgun with "00" buckshot, and killed him. The prisoners were real upset about it. That could have been any one of them, because evidently these guards would taunt them when they were out on detail and say, "I could just blow you away, say you were trying to run."

I was torn by all this, because I did respect the prisoners' position and many times thought of saying, stick me in the stockade, I ain't going to cooperate because I don't believe in this. But my fear always prevailed. I also felt it was good for me to be there because there were a few other guys who were not too bad, but there were a lot of bad guards. So I helped these guys by being a fellow human being, by not piling more stuff on, but indeed trying to lighten the load that they were carrying. For many years I didn't know if anyone realized this. And recently the "Presidio 27," as they came to be known, had a reunion and told me they recognized my efforts.

Terry Hallinan, a lawyer for the Presidio 27, contacted me to ask me to be a defense witness at the mutiny trial, and I agreed. I talked to him about the conditions and the things that had gone on and what had happened, and he seemed to think those things needed to be brought out. The trial was front page news, day after day and over and over again the Army looked ridiculous. People were protesting more and more, and I think the Army pretty much had their fill of this bad publicity. I was real fortunate in that. If this had been a more isolated incident, I think they would have hung me. If this would have happened six months earlier, I wouldn't have had a prayer. Or if it had happened in Texas instead of San Francisco.

I wasn't political, I was just a guy who found myself in this position where the psychic brutality was more than I could handle. It was turds in the showers, the lousy conditions, the overcrowding, the brutality of killing people, the psychic games, it was a pressure cooker, the place was incredible. It's affected me to this day, 20 years later it still affects me . . . and God only knows what might have been my life otherwise.

BRAGG BRIEFS

DECEMBER 71   DONATIONS

VOL. 4   no 8

THIS IS YOUR PERSONAL PROPERTY (AR 210-10).
ANYONE WHO TRIES TO TAKE IT FROM YOU IS COMMITTING A CRIME.

DARE TO **UNITE**

ORGANIZE

BRAGG

GI
AGAINST THE

VOL. 3   NO. 11   JANUARY 1971

GI's United

Joe Bangert

Roy Barrington

John Berk

Chuck Brown

Ben Chitty

David Cortright

Paul Cox

Bill Davis

Ricky Dodd

Jabiya Dragonsun

Nate Goldshlag

Ruben Gomez

Harry Haines

Dave Henry

Dave Hettick

Dave Hockabout

Larry Holmes

Allan Horn

Michael Hovey

Ron Jacko

Terry Klug

Steve Morse

Hal Muskat

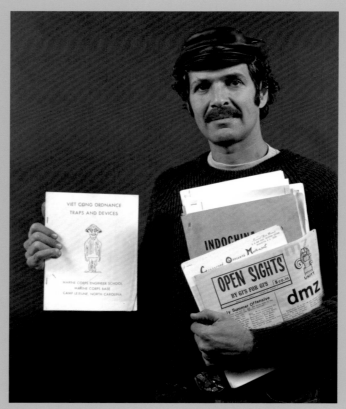

Jim Packer

Kim Scipes

Dan Siebens

George Silver

Lamont Steptoe

Dennis Stout

Jack Tracey

Richard Valentine

Tahan Jones

Stephanie Atkinson

Erik Larsen

By the time the Persian Gulf War began in January of 1991, 2,500 servicemen and women had applied for conscientious objector status. Like their Vietnam counterparts, many spoke out publicly against the Gulf War, risking court-martial and imprisonment. Twenty-six of those charged with disloyalty, AWOL, and a variety of other charges were adopted by Amnesty International as prisoners of conscience. Sentences have varied from three months to two years for those already tried and convicted. At the time of this writing many more await court-martial.

    The reasons given by these resisters for their opposition to the Gulf War are strikingly similar to those given by veterans who opposed the Vietnam War.

AGENT REPORT
(AR 381-130; PM 30-17)

1. NAME OF SUBJECT OR TITLE OF INCIDENT	2. DATE SUBMITTED
GIs United Against the War (GIUAW) Re: DELANO, Lewis A.	23 October 1969
	3. CONTROL SYMBOL OR FILE NUMBER
	ZB 50 44 91

4. REPORT OF FINDINGS

(LOCAL AGENCY)   On 23 October 1969 , the following information pertaining to SUBJECT was obtained from the records of the Provost Marshal's Office:

REFERRED DCSPER LED

GROUP - 3
DOWNGRADED AT 12 YEAR INTERVALS:
NOT AUTOMATICALLY DECLASSIFIED.

208

5. TYPED NAME AND ORGANIZATION OF SPECIAL AGENT	6. SIGNATURE OF SPECIAL AGENT
GEORGE W. BUCKINGHAM, 111th MI Group (IV)	George W Buck

DA FORM 341   REPLACES WD AGO FORM 341, 1 JUN 47, WHICH MAY BE USED.

BIOGRAPHIES

Paul Atwood. Enlisted Marine Corps 1965–67. Infantry, participated in the 1965 invasion of Dominican Republic. Refused to go to Vietnam. Imprisoned and discharged early. Currently a Professor of American History and veteran activist in the Boston area.

Joe Bangert. Enlisted Marine Corps 1967–70. Served in Vietnam 1968. Formed anti-war group with other GIs in his unit. Involved in sabotage to undermine the war effort. Part of an onboard strike aboard the USS Bexar (a transport ship used for bringing marines back to the U.S.); upon entry into San Francisco Harbor, draped a huge peace sign made from stolen bedsheets over the side of the ship. Former director of Massachusetts Agent Orange program. Has returned to Vietnam four times and is presently a consultant for companies interested in doing business with Vietnam. Lives on Cape Cod with his wife and two children.

Roy Barrington. Enlisted Army 1969–71. Infantry in Vietnam 1969–70. Made peace signs out of shaving cream on a landing zone in Cambodia where a battalion commander was to arrive. AWOL after Vietnam, court-martialed, reduced in rank from sergeant to private first class. Received General Discharge. Active member of VVAW-Anti-Imperialist in the Seattle area. Chained himself to the gate of the Naval Reserve Station in Seattle to protest reserve troop shipments to the Persian Gulf; recently lost his job as a result of protest work against the Gulf War.

John Berk. Enlisted Army 1966–71. Delayed enlistment in order to go to medical school. Active duty 1970–71. Filed CO application prior to active duty. While on active duty at Fort Bragg involved with Concerned Officers Movement and *Bragg Briefs*, GI underground newspaper. Helped organize FTA show (alternative USO tour) at Fort Bragg. Filed successful lawsuit against the Army for discharge related to CO application. Released from active duty after serving only six months. Currently a dentist in the San Francisco Bay area.

Dave Blalock. Enlisted Army 1968–71 Served in Vietnam 1969. Active in "GIs & WACs United Against the War" at Fort McClellan, Alabama and *Left Face*, GI underground newspaper. Following discharge worked with United States Servicemen's Fund. Defendant in the 1989 flag burning case sent to the U.S. Supreme Court. Union organizer and active in organizing GI resistance to Persian Gulf War. Currently active with VVAW-Anti-Imperialist, living in Houston, Texas.

Roger Broomfield. Drafted Army 1967–69. MP, Presidio Stockade guard. Testified at mutiny trial on behalf of the Presidio 27 against the wishes of the U.S. military. Currently working as a carpenter in the San Francisco area.

Chuck Brown. Drafted Army 1968–69. Deserted to Sweden. Still lives in Sweden where he is working on his doctorate in social anthropology.

Ben Chitty. Enlisted Navy 1965–69. Served on USS Richmond K. Turner in Gulf of Tonkin. Refused Shore Patrol duty after the assassination of Martin Luther King, Jr., in April 1968. Currently active with VVAW, Inc. in New York area, working as a military counsellor and speaking to students about military service and the Vietnam War.

Charlie Clements. Enlisted as a cadet in the Air Force Academy where he graduated second in his class in 1967. Served as a C–130 pilot in SE Asia until the invasion of Cambodia when he refused to fly further missions, resulting in psychiatric hospitalization and medical discharge with a 10% mental disability. *Witness to War* is the title of an Academy Award winning documentary film and book describing the journey of conscience that led him to work as a physician in areas of El Salvador bombed by the planes he once flew. Currently the director of SatelLife with the International Physicians for the Prevention of Nuclear War in Boston.

Dave Cline. Drafted Army 1967–69. Served as a combat infantryman in Vietnam where he was wounded twice, receiving Purple Hearts and a Bronze Star. Upon return, became active in the GI anti-war movement, helping to publish the *Fatigue Press*, GI underground newspaper at Fort Hood, Texas. Currently national coordinator of VVAW, Inc. and president of New Jersey chapter of Veterans for Peace, and a loyal union officer, living with his wife and children in New Jersey.

Gerry Condon. Enlisted Army 1967–75. Green Beret, refused to go to Vietnam, deserted to Canada and Sweden in 1969, returned to Canada in 1972 and to the U.S. in 1975. Now a peace activist living in the San Francisco area and currently working on the defense of Erik Larsen and Tahan Jones, two Persian Gulf GI resisters.

David Cortright. Drafted Army 1968–71. GI organizing at Fort Hamilton, New York and Fort Bliss, Texas. One of a group of GIs who filed federal court suit against Army, *Cortright V. Resor*, alleging that transfers, work assignments and changes in duty were an attempt to suppress First Amendment rights. Authored book, *Soldiers in Revolt,* a major study of GI resistance during the Vietnam War, and *Left Face*, an examination of soldier resistance and trade unions in the armies of many countries. Former Executive Director of SANE and currently Visiting Fellow at the Institute for International Peace Studies at the University of Notre Dame, finishing a book on the impact of the peace movement during the 1980's.

Paul Cox. Enlisted Marine Corps 1968–72. Served in combat in Vietnam 1969–70. After Vietnam service helped found *Rage*, GI underground newspaper at Camp Lejeune, North Carolina and alternative bookstore. Currently employed as a civil engineer in the San Francisco area, and active with the Veterans Speakers Alliance, an organization that sends veterans into high schools and colleges to talk about their war experiences.

Bill Davis. Enlisted Air Force 1966–70. Served with Tactical Airlift Squadron in Vietnam and Tactical Air Recon, a component of the Automated Battlefield Project in Thailand. General non-compliance with orders; AWOL after Vietnam. Currently active with VVAW, Inc. in Chicago area, working as a UPS truck mechanic and union steward.

Skip Delano. Enlisted Army 1967–70. Served one year in Vietnam. Co-founded *Left Face* in 1969, GI underground newspaper at Fort McClellan, Alabama, published until 1972. Court-martialed for running a stop sign. Received several Article 15s in an attempt to reduce his rank from sergeant to private. Currently a political activist living in New York City, working toward a Ph.D. in American History and lecturing in universities and high school schools about the GI movement.

Carl Dix. Enlisted Army 1968–72. One of the Fort Lewis 6, refused to go to Vietnam, spent 18 months in Leavenworth Federal Prison. Founding member and currently national spokesperson of the Revolutionary Communist Party, based in New York City.

Ricky Dodd. Drafted Army 1968–70. AWOL, Court-martialed, imprisoned for one year in Presidio Stockade. Participant in the Presidio 27 Mutiny, a sit-down strike by prisoners. Transferred to Leavenworth Federal Prison for additional one-year sentence. Received Dishonorable Discharge. Currently lives in Washington State and is happily married with two children, working as a drug and alcohol counsellor.

Jabiya Dragonsun (Julius Williams). Enlisted Army 1967–69. Passive resistance: general non-compliance with orders in Vietnam. Actively spoke against the war at peace rallies while stationed at Fort Carson, Colorado. Currently a veteran activist in the Philadelphia area and writes poetry concerned with human issues.

Donald Duncan. Drafted Army 1954–64. Served 1 1/2 years in Vietnam with Green Beret Special Forces. Resigned in opposition to the war. Following military service became outspoken anti-war advocate, authored *The New Legions*, a book critical of the military and U.S. policies in Vietnam. Returned to Vietnam in 1968 as a journalist for *Ramparts* magazine. Currently working as a Director of Employment & Training for a federal jobs training program in Indiana.

Clarence Fitch. Enlisted Marine Corps 1966–69. Served in Vietnam in 1968. Involved in GI organizing efforts while still on active duty, especially in fighting for the rights of black servicemen. Became a veteran activist following the war, serving as East Coast coordinator for VVAW, Inc. Died of AIDS May 7, 1990.

Steve Fournier. Enlisted Marine Corps 1966–68. Served in Vietnam 1967–68. Wounded twice, given a medical retirement. Spoke publicly at an anti-war rally in Boston in 1968, two weeks before being discharged from the military. Student leader of Vietnam Moratorium Committee at Merrimack College 1969–70. Currently owns and operates The Book Review, a bookstore in Falmouth, Maine and active in national leadership of Veterans for Peace.

Nate Goldshlag. Drafted Army 1970–72. Working with the Progressive Labor Party, allowed himself to be drafted to organize against the military from within. Stationed in Germany, worked on *Fight Back*, GI underground newspaper in Frankfurt. Active in the movement to oppose U.S. foreign policy in Central America in the 1980s. Currently a member of the Smedley Butler Brigade of Veterans For Peace, and working as an electronics engineer in the Boston area.

Ruben Gomez. Drafted Army 1966–69. Drafted at age 26 with four kids. Served one year in Vietnam 1967–68. Wounded on Ho Chi Minh's birthday. AWOL two times (8 days and six months) following Vietnam service. Received two special courts-martial. Reduced in rank. Has been active with VFW Bill Motto Post in Santa Cruz and Veterans for Peace. Returned to Vietnam in 1989 to help establish medical clinic. Presently working as Santa Cruz representative of Project Hearts and Minds, sending medicine and medical supplies to Vietnam and Cambodia.

Peter Hagerty. Harvard University ROTC, Navy 1968–69. Assigned to the USS Lloyd Thomas. Refused to signify forward gunmount as combat ready and refused to sail with the ship when ordered to the Gulf of Tonkin. After discharge, in August 1970, traveled to Vietnam as part of the Lawyers Military Defense Committee. Currently active with Veterans for Peace in Maine. With his wife Martha Tracy, is a co-founder and co-director of Soviet-American Woolens, established in 1985 to promote better U.S./Soviet relations through trade. Has worked with Soviet veterans of the Afghanistan War around issues of Post-Traumatic Stress Disorder (PTSD).

Harry Haines. Drafted Army 1969–71. Active with *aboveground*, GI underground newspaper at Fort Carson, Colorado. Served in convalescent center in Cam Ranh Bay, Vietnam, engaged in passive resistance: general non-compliance with orders. Currently teaches in the Department of Communication at Trinity University in San Antonio, Texas, and has written about the protrayal of the Vietnam War and Vietnam veterans in film and television.

Dave Henry. Enlisted (Draft-motivated) Air Force 1970–72. Active with GI Alliance while stationed at McChord Air Force Base in Washington State, and with the *Lewis-McChord Free Press*, GI underground newspaper at nearby Fort Lewis. Discharged early and received lifetime ban from Fort Lewis and McChord. Currently Safety Director, Hazardous Material/Environmental Remediation for environmental company in the Seattle area.

Dave Hettick. Enlisted Army 1969. After returning from Vietnam worked on *Bragg Briefs*, GI underground newspaper at Fort Bragg, North Carolina. Currently working as a lawyer in the San Francisco Bay area.

Oliver Hirsch. Enlisted Air Force 1966–68. AWOL, became part of the "Nine for Peace." Was forced to waive any veteran's benefits, was banned from military installations and discharged with a "general under other than honorable conditions." Now living in New York City with his two teen-age daughters. Currently performing in New York clubs with his band STURM&TWANG, playing the seditious country music which he writes. Unrepentant.

Dave Hockabout. Enlisted Air Force 1970–73. Served in the Philippines. Filed for CO, organized anti-war demonstration at Williams Air Force Base near Phoenix, Arizona. Currently a staff member for the Thomas Merton Center, a peace and justice center in Pittsburgh, Pennsylvania, and a member of Veterans for Peace.

Larry Holmes. Drafted Army 1971–72. Anti-war agitation while at Fort Dix, New Jersey. During 8-month AWOL spoke publicly against the war and became involved in the American Servicemen's Union. Spent one month in Fort Dix stockade and received Undesirable Discharge. Currently active with Workers World Party in New York City.

Allan Horn. Enlisted Coast Guard 1969 for four years; discharged in 1971 as a "violent person," resulting from an incident onboard the U.S.C.G. Cutter Minnetonka. Tried, unsuccessfully, to organize mutiny in advance of initiation ceremony in connection with crossing the International Dateline, in which he and other known anti-war sailors had been threatened with severe hazing and physical abuse. Currently Secretary of the San Francisco Chapter #505 of Vietnam Veterans of America, member of Veterans Speakers Alliance, founder of San Mateo Nuclear Weapons Freeze, now SANE/FREEZE, and working in a family insurance brokerage in Burlingame, California.

Michael Hovey. Enlisted Navy 1971. Former seminarian. Used position as a military drug counsellor to help sailors get out of the military. Stationed in Japan, where he often visited the Peace Park and museum in Nagasaki, site of atomic bombing by the U.S. in World War II. Filed for and was awarded CO status just after the Vietnam War ended. Currently a Ph.D. student in Peace Studies at Syracuse University in New York.

Terry Irvin. Drafted Army 1970–71. Worked with GI Alliance and *Lewis-McChord Free Press*, GI underground newspaper at Fort Lewis, Washington. Arrested for passing out the Declaration of Independence on base on 4th of July. Currently living in central Illinois, where he is President of Champion Travel, father of two kids and a member of VVAW-Anti-Imperialist.

Ron Jacko. Enlisted Marine Corps 1968–90. Deserted to Canada. Returned to the U.S. in 1990, was given an "Other Than Honorable" Discharge and received $61.50 in back pay. Currently lives in Toronto, Canada where he manages a health food store.

Alan Klein. Enlisted Air Force 1966–67. AWOL, received General Discharge. Currently Professor of Sociology-Anthropology at Northeastern University in Boston.

Terry Klug. Enlisted Army 1966–71. Refused to go to Vietnam; went AWOL to Europe in May of 1967. Established RITA/ACT (Resisters in the Army, a Paris-based GI anti-war group) with Dick Perrin and Max Watts. Returned to the U.S. January 1969, charged with desertion. Received Dishonorable Discharge and sentenced to three years in Leavenworth Federal Prison. Involved in June 1969 rebellion at Fort Dix Stockade ("Ft. Dix 38"). Found not-guilty of charges related to Fort Dix rebellion at second court-martial. Spent 14 months in Leavenworth. Currently a member of Workers World Party and recording secretary of Local 241, Transport Workers Union of America, AFL-CIO, in New York City.

Howard Levy. Enlisted Army 1965-69. Army doctor, refused to train Green Beret medics. Sentenced to three years in Leavenworth Federal Prison. Following prison term worked with United States Servicemen's Fund, an organization providing material aid to the GI movement, and wrote the book *Going To Jail*, with David Miller, the first person to burn his draft card. Currently a doctor of dermatology at Lincoln Hospital in the Bronx, New York.

Keith Mather. Drafted Army 1967–85. AWOL, participant in the "Nine for Peace" and Presidio 27 Mutiny, a sit-down strike by prisoners. Escaped from the Presidio stockade in San Francisco and deserted to Canada. Secretly returned to the U.S. in 1980. Arrested in 1984. Imprisoned and court-martialed after serving $4^1/_2$ months, and discharged from military in 1985. Currently a contractor and veteran activist in the San Francisco area.

Steve Morse. Enlisted Army 1969–71 (Officially discharged 1973) Quaker upbringing, received CO status at age 18. Civil rights and anti-war activist; distributed GI-oriented anti-war newspaper *The Bond*. Enlisted to organize GIs from within the Army. May 1970, court-martialed for distributing anti-war leaflets, Fort Lewis, Washington. Two weeks into four-month sentence, shipped to Vietnam. Saw light combat in an armored unit, and continued to disseminate resistance viewpoint and literature. After four months in-country, transferred to Fort Riley, Kansas. July 1971, court-martialed again for publicizing rebellions on base. Served $3^1/_2$ months in stockade, including 7-weeks solitary confinement. Received Bad Conduct Discharge. Currently a community activist and member of

the Veterans Speakers Alliance, working as a journeyman in the building trades, and residing in Oakland, California with his wife and their two teen-age daughters.

Hal Muskat. Enlisted Army 1965–70 (including 6 mos. bad time in stockade). Stationed in Germany, refused to go to Vietnam. Court-martialed twice for distributing unauthorized literature while on base at Fort Dix, New Jersey. Currently a peace/veteran activist and co-founder of Veterans Speakers Alliance and United Bay Area Veterans Against War in the Middle East, father of three in the San Francisco area, trying to open a bakery/cafe.

Jim Packer. Enlisted as a career soldier, Marine Corps 1966–71. Officer Candidates School. Served in Vietnam 1967–68, with 11th Engineers, installing minefields in DMZ. Received Purple Heart and Bronze Star with V. Joined Concerned Officers Movement (COM) upon invasion of Cambodia, 1970. National Secretary for COM. Repeatedly threatened with court-martial as form of harassment; sideburns too long, being out of uniform, late for duty station. Stripped of security clearance, and at one time was the most senior first lieutenant in the Marine Corps (repeatedly passed over for promotion to captain). Currently a lawyer and active in Smedley Butler Brigade, Boston chapter of Veterans for Peace.

Greg Payton. Drafted Army 1967–69. Received three courts-martial for a variety of charges, including AWOL, assault and disrespect to an officer. Involved in the 1968 prison riot at Long Binh Jail in South Vietnam. Currently an active member of Vietnam Veterans Against the War, Inc. in the New Jersey area. Made return trip to Vietnam in 1988. Traveled to South Africa in 1990 on behalf of VVAW. Member of Executive Committee of War Resisters League in New York City. Works as a consultant for substance abuse and AIDS training.

Tom Roberts. Enlisted Army 1967-70. Served with Psychological Operations in Vietnam 1967–68, attached to Second ARVN Armored Calvary Squadron in Mekong Delta. Co-founder and editor of *aboveground*, GI underground newspaper at Fort Carson, Colorado. Currently a personal injury and Workers' Compensation lawyer for individual claimants and plaintiffs in the Denver area.

Randy Rowland. Enlisted Army 1967–69. AWOL 45 days while preparing second Conscientious Objector application. Imprisoned in Presidio Stockade, San Francisco. Participant in Presidio 27 Mutiny, a sit-down strike by prisoners. Court-martialed, sentenced to total of 21 months, of which he served 18 months before being released from United States Disciplinary Barracks in Leavenworth. Received Dishonorable Discharge. Currently a Registered Nurse in Seattle, and editor of *Storm Warning!*, the publication of Vietnam VVAW-Anti-Imperialist.

Susan Schnall. Enlisted Naval Reserves 1965–69. (Active duty 1967–69) Navy nurse stationed in San Francisco Bay area. Along with pilot friend, flew over military installations dropping leaflets announcing GI and Veterans' Peace March, and spoke at the rally in uniform. Court-martialed. After military service worked with United States Servicemen's Fund, an organization providing material aid to the GI movement. Also worked with the Medical Committee for Human Rights and Medical Aid to Indochina organizations. Currently works as an associate director in hospital administration in a long term care facility in the New York area, and active in the field of rights for the disabled.

Kim Scipes. Enlisted Marine Corps 1969–73. Assigned to a Human Rights Program at Marine Corps Air Station in Yuma, Arizona, formed in response to racial tension throughout the Marines Corps. (Every major Marine base in world had suffered at least one case of racial violence by 1971.) Part of a three-man team that worked to confront institutional (promotions, etc.) and personal racism among officers and enlisted personnel, and later to assist those harassed around drug useage, and those generally resisting Marine Corps program. Has been a member of Veterans Speakers Alliance in San Francisco area, and currently finishing a graduate program in the Politics of Alternative Development Strategies at the Institute of Social Studies in The Hague, The Netherlands.

Bill Short. Drafted Army 1968–69. Attended NCOC school, U.S. Military Infantry War College, Fort Benning, Georgia. Squad leader and platoon sergeant, 1st Infantry Division, Vietnam 1969. Court-martialed twice in Vietnam for refusing to fight. Initially charged with leading a conspiracy to mutiny. Served two months of a 7 month sentence in Long Binh Stockade, South Vietnam. Received General Discharge. Currently artist and photographer living in Cambridge, and a veteran activist working for the defense of Erik Larsen and Tahan Jones.

Dan Siebens. Drafted Army 1969–71. Refused to take loyalty oath, refused to take a weapon in basic training. Orders to Vietnam cancelled for investigation into subversive activities. Currently lives in Madison, Wisconsin and works as a machinist.

George Silver. Enlisted Army 1967–73. Served with a Long Range Reconnaisance Team in Vietnam 1968–69. Decided to "quit" the war after an orphanage and village befriended by his team were bombed and destroyed by American forces. Received 100% disability from military for non-controllable chronic epilepsy, resulting from wounds sustained in Vietnam, and from Post-Traumatic Stress Disorder (PTSD). Currently a writer and sculptor living in Portland, Oregon, and a member of VVAW-Anti-Imperialist.

Steve Spund. Enlisted Marine Corps 1965–66. Refused to go to Vietnam, AWOL two times. Put in brig, suffered physical abuse by Marine guards. Transferred to psychiatric ward of hospital after threatening to commit suicide. Given General Discharge Under Honorable Conditions. Now married and living in San Francisco, working for an information specialist company.

Andy Stapp. Enlisted Army 1966–68. Enlisted to organize from within the Army. Court-martialed three times for anti-war activities. Founder of the American Servicemen's Union and publisher of *The Bond*, GI underground newspaper. Author of *Up Against the Brass*. Currently a schoolteacher and contributing editor to *Workers World*, a socialist newspaper in New York City.

Lamont Steptoe. Enlisted Army 1968–71. Participated in mass defection from Infantry Officer Candidate's School. Served as a dog handler in Vietnam for 16 months. Consistent outspoken critic of racism within the military. Organized demonstration in Vietnam with black GIs to commemorate the death of Malcolm X. Threatened with court-martial. Now a poet and Theater Manager and Poetry Consultant for the Spoken Word series at the Painted Bride Theater in Philadelphia.

Curt Stocker. Enlisted Army 1967–70. Served with Psychological Operations in Vietnam. Co-published *aboveground*, GI newspaper at Fort Carson, Colorado. Today lives in the Denver area and works in cable TV.

Dennis Stout. Enlisted Army 1966–69. Served in Vietnam with the 101st Airborne 1966–67. Recommended for two Bronze Stars, Silver Star, Distinguish Service Cross and Battlefield Commission to 2nd Lieutenant. While stationed in Vietnam, tried to report 14 war crimes, including the killing and torture of innocent civilians, and gang rape. Received personal threat against his life. Immediately upon discharge went public with allegations of war crimes and again threatened by military investigators. Currently a member of Veterans For Peace, crisis counsellor for spouse abuse in New Hampshire and active around humanitarian issues in Central America.

Jack Tracey. Enlisted Navy 1969–72. Served as radio operator in Vietnam. Became involved in VVAW five days after returning from Vietnam, while still on active duty, and helped organize Lexington to Boston anti-war march, May 1971. Court-martialed for being AWOL and spent 21st birthday in the brig. Assisted by Legal In-Service Project, which he later joined, assisting active duty GIs and veterans with legal assistance and counseling. Currently works in electronic monitoring of people under house arrest. Married, with three children, he now resides in South Florida where he and his wife are active in grant writing and social action. He is active with Veterans for Peace and Vietnam Veterans of America, and recently worked with issues around the Persian Gulf War.

John Tuma. Enlisted Army 1969–72. Served in Vietnam 1971 as an interrogator, trained in Vietnamese. Refused to torture Viet Cong prisoners. Currently works in the Archeology Lab at the University of Massachusetts in Boston.

Richard Valentine. Enlisted Army 1968–72. Served as a door gunner in Vietnam 1968–70. After returning from Vietnam, worked with *FTA*, GI underground newspaper at Fort Knox, Kentucky. Currently living in Seattle and finally ending his post-war era.

Mike Wong. Drafted Army 1969–75. AWOL, deserted to Canada. Returned to U.S. in 1975. Political activist since 1984, involved in two Democratic presidential campaigns. Former board member of Sacramento SANE/FREEZE. Currently active with United Bay Area Veterans Against War and Veterans Speakers Alliance. Served as a draft and military counsellor during the Persian Gulf War. Employed as a social worker for developmentally delayed children in the San Francisco area.

★   ★   ★

Stephanie Atkinson. Enlisted Army Reserves 1984–90. Failed to report to active duty for activation to the Persian Gulf, October 1990. While AWOL for two weeks publicly spoke against the Persian Gulf War. Charged with desertion and missing troop movement. Arrested and confined at Fort Knox, Kentucky. Received Other than Honorable Discharge. Currently an intern with the Youth and Militarism Project of the the American Friends Service Committee in Philadelphia.

Erik Larsen. Enlisted Marine Corps Reserves 1986–present. August 1990 publicly declared himself a conscientious objector and informed the military he would refuse to be sent to Saudi Arabia if called. CO application was denied. Traveled worldwide to publicly speak against the Persian Gulf War. Charged with "desertion in a time of war," and upon reporting to a Naval base in San Francisco was handcuffed and taken to Camp Lejeune, North Carolina. Threatened with death penalty, then seven years in prison. November 1991 sentenced to six months in the brig.

Tahan Jones. Enlisted Marine Corps Reserves 1987–present. Joined Marine Reserves at age 17. Filed CO application October 1990 and began speaking in high schools, colleges and anti-war rallies against the Persian Gulf War. Went UA (unauthorized absence) just after his unit was activated in February 1991. Turned himself in May 1991 and was taken to Camp Lejeune, North Carolina, where he is threatened with seven years in prison. As of this writing he is still awaiting court-martial.

GLOSSARY

ARVN   The Army of the Republic of Vietnam, or the South Vietnamese Army, U.S. allies

AWOL   absent without leave

Article 15   Uniform Code of Military Justice. Non-judicial punishment for minor disciplinary infractions without going through regular criminal court process. Can result in extra duty, confinement to quarters, reduction in rank and pay.

B-52   US heavy bomber

Bloods   term used by black soldiers to refer to themselves

brig   Navy or Marine prison

CID   Criminal Investigation Division

C-130   transport and air cargo plane

claymore   anti-personnel mine carried by infantry

CO   commanding officer; or conscientious objection

court-martial   military trial

DMZ   demilitarized zone separating North and South Vietnam at the 17th parallel

fragging   murder or attempted murder of US military officers by US troops; derived from fragmentation grenade, a grenade often used in the assaults

GI   government issue

hooch   Slang used by GIs to describe their living quarters or Vietnamese homes.

in-country   term used by GIs to refer to being in Vietnam

KIA   killed in action

medevac   medical evacuation by helicopter

MI   Military Intelligence

MP   Military Police

My Lai   March 1968 masscre by a U.S. infantry company of more than 300 South Vietnamese civilians in My Lai village, made public in 1969.

NCO   non-commissioned officer, i.e. sergeant

NVA   North Vietnamese Army

Phoenix Program   covert CIA campaign designed to wipe out the NLF's (Viet Cong) rural structure, resulting in the imprisonment, torture and murder of tens of thousands of Vietnamese

platoon   approximately 45 men assigned to a company (3–4 platoons per company); in Vietnam average platoon size was 25–30 men

PsyOps   Psychological Operations; military propaganda unit

recon   reconnaissance, small scout patrol to search for enemy activity

ROTC   Reserve Officers' Training Corps

RTO   radio telephone operator ("radioman")

SDS   Students for a Democratic Society

stockade   Army prison

Tet   The Chinese and Vietnamese lunar new year; in many cases used to denote the 1968 Tet Offensive, a major offensive by the North Vietnamese, generally viewed as a turning point in the war

VA   Veterans Administration

VVAW   Vietnam Veterans Against the War

VC or **Viet Cong**   American term for members of National Liberation Front (NFL), considered derogatory by many Vietnamese

The World   Term used by soldiers to refer to the United States or home

Published by active-duty servicepeople from Fort lewis, McChord AFB and Bremerton Naval Shipyard.

Donation 25¢   July 1971

UT DECLARATION

The
American colonists'
DECLARATION
OF
INDEPENDENCE
4 July 1776

A MATTER OF CONSCIENCE

Each of the photographs and oral histories of former GI resisters compiled in this book bears witness to difficult individual choices and actions the veterans confronted and sustained with strong personal convictions during the Vietnam War. Considered together, these portraits and histories represent a larger voice of dissent that erupted from within the ranks of the U.S. military, and came to frustrate our leaders' ability to fight a war that many Americans believed was unjust. From seemingly small individual acts, such as that of Steve Fournier speaking at an anti-war rally two weeks before he was to be discharged from the military; or Dr. Howard Levy's refusal to train Green Beret medics—a public case that became a cause celebre—thousands of soldiers spoke up and acted against the war that tragically divided our nation.

In the years following the 1982 dedication of the Vietnam Veterans Memorial, an event intended as an act of healing for this country, we watched as Hollywood films, books, and television documentaries revisited the war and its aftermath, intently looking for a mention of the GI dissent we knew to be pervasive during the conflict. The Vietnam War has been scrutinized and analyzed, but the retrospection has been narrowly defined. There can be no one experience, no one truth that comes to represent the Vietnam experience; so we wondered how a full accounting of the war could ever be told without adding the story of GI resistance. Dissent within the military's own ranks is a powerful chapter in the history of the war, and one that may help us better understand why the Vietnam War continues to haunt our nation.

This project is our attempt to help fill a void that still exists. Our 58 interviews collected over a five-year period, represent only a fraction of the stories of GI resistance that might be told; they speak for the many more thousands of GIs who shared their feelings, but did not feel able to act. In gathering the interviews, we purposely sought out veterans who could represent a broad range of the types of resistance that gave the GI movement its momentum. Many of our contacts came by word of mouth—people connected to the network of peace veterans who have remained active since the end of the war. In addition, a number of anti-war veterans groups helped us by providing their member mailing lists, and by putting notices of our project in their newsletters and newspapers. We were also able to identify some of the more prominent figures in the GI movement through important resources such as David Cortright's book, *Soldiers In Revolt* and James Robert Hayes' thesis, *The War Within a War.*

When we arrived for interviews—lugging along tape recorders and a portable photographic studio—our only prior contact with the veteran was often just a short telephone conversation, and our knowledge of the veteran's experience sketchy. Yet each veteran willingly shared intimate, often painful details of his or her life with us. We approached every interview with a certain amount of apprehension; often fearing their story would strike an emotional chord in us. Indeed, many of the interviews were draining, yet remarkably moving. There were times when we could no longer bear to hear or think about Vietnam. But we always found ourselves enthusiastically recounting the story we had just heard, and feeling a renewed inspiration from the strength of the veteran's words and convictions.

We tried to make the two to four hour interviews as relaxed as possible. Even though we had specific questions for all the veterans about their lives and their active resistance to the war, we wanted them to feel free to roam through memories at their own pace. We

were interested in drawing forth *their own stories* as they remembered them, as they would wish for them to be passed on to another
generation. In the process of editing the taped interviews, we often
consulted with the veterans to assure that the statements accompa-
nying their photographic portraits remained true to the essence of
the interview. Thus, we sought to imbue our work with a
collaborative spirit, a mutually contractual process, of which the
veterans were an integral part. The same approach was used in
creating the photographic portraits, which were taken at the end of
each interview. We asked each veteran to bring some objects of
personal value or significance to the portrait session. These objects
were presented as an offering of who they were, or who they have
become. Some felt they had nothing to offer but themselves, and
that, after all, was the most valuable thing they could give.

William Short and Willa Seidenberg
December 1, 1991

AFTERWORD

I was first introduced to William Short and Willa Seidenberg's *A Matter of Conscience* project in 1986. At the time, Kevin Bowen, Co-Director of the William Joiner Center for the Study of War and Social Consequences at the University of Massachusetts, Boston, was assisting Philip Brookman and me at the Washington Project for the Arts. He kindly suggested ways we might enrich a representation of Vietnam veteran artists in a program we were organizing entitled: *War and Memory: In the Aftermath of Vietnam* (a three-month, multi-disciplinary program of visual art, commissioned installations, photography, film, video, literature, theater, music and public discussions presented in the nation's capitol in 1987). Among the many Vietnam veteran filmmakers, poets, painters and photographers Bowen offered for review, was William Short, then a new member of Boston's artistic community.

Short had begun a project documenting GI dissent and resistance within the military services during the Vietnam years. I called him to arrange a studio visit and soon viewed the first of these stunning photographic portraits. The images moved me with a visual and emotional power equal to August Sander's epic work in Germany. Side by side with each image were the compelling oral histories Short and Seidenberg had compiled with their subjects, unvarnished stories resonating with a clarity of voice and trust that recalls Studs Terkel interviewing and editing at his best.

The first eight completed portraits and oral histories from *A Matter of Conscience* were included in WPA's 1987 *War and Memory* exhibition. Short and Seidenberg kept working, clearly intending their project to grow in order to better document this underknown chapter in the history of the Vietnam War. I looked forward to encountering their work again in its expanded form.

Upon returning to my alma mater in 1989, I was interested to find that a class was being taught at Phillips Academy entitled: *A Hard Rain is Gonna Fall: The Literature, Music and Film of the Vietnam War*. Its creator and instructor, Seth Bardo, was in fact using *Unwinding the Vietnam War—From War Into Peace*, (the anthology of writings WPA published in conjunction with its *War and Memory* project) as a textbook for this class. William Short came to a session of Bardo's class that year, invited as a visiting speaker sponsored by the Addison Gallery. That evening he shared an enlarged version of *A Matter of Conscience* with Andover students. An amazing discussion ensued between two generations of Americans during those hours, one that focused on the tremendous complexities involved in a love of country, duty, and service, and the exercise of personal conscience. The riveting vitality of that conversation prompted my expanded commitment to Short and Seidenberg's art. Others have joined in that commitment by generously funding the travel and production work necessary to bring this project to fruition.

After being exhibited in the museum's galleries, the work will enter the Addison's permanent collection, joining other compelling bodies of Vietnam era images created by photographers such as Dick Durrance (PA '61), Sal Lopes, and Bill Burke. We trust *A Matter of Conscience* will be a rich artistic and educational resource for this school and our colleagues in the field of American art.

Jock Reynolds, Director
December 1, 1991

ACKNOWLEDGEMENTS

This artist book is published on the occasion of the Addison Gallery exhibition, *A Matter of Conscience* and *Vietnam Revisited*, photographs by William Short and oral histories by Willa Seidenberg and William Short, on public view from January 24 through March 15, 1992. Short and Seidenberg's art is presented in conjunction with an exhibition of *The Black Paintings*, by Le Tri Dung. All three showings have been scheduled to coincide with Phillips Academy's winter term course: *A Hard Rain is Gonna Fall: The Literature, Film and Music of the Vietnam War.*

The exhibitions, artist book, and educational programs have been supported with generous grants and gifts from the Massachusetts Cultural Council, a state agency; the Addison Gallery—Edward Elson Artist in Residence fund; the LEF Foundation; the William Joiner Foundation; the William Joiner Center for the Study of War and Social Consequences at the University of Massachusetts, Boston; the Polaroid Corporation; the Cambridge Arts Council; Color Services; Cambridge Camera; the Lucius & Eva Eastman Fund; Mel and Elenore Seidenberg; and Judy Ullman.

William Short and Willa Seidenberg would like to acknowledge the encouragement and assistance offered them by Sally Abugov, the staff of the Addison Gallery, Paul Atwood, Erik Baier, Kevin Bowen, Bradford College, Dave Cline, Paul Cox, Skip Delano, Tod Ensign, Roena Group, David Hunt, Kelly Kildow, Lucy Lippard, John Luvender, Nathan and Joan Lyons and the staff of the Visual Studies Workshop, Gerry Nicosia, Randy Rowland, Tatiana Schreiber, Veterans for Peace, Vietnam Veterans Against the War-Anti-Imperialist, Vietnam Veterans Against the War, Inc., many friends across the country who generously provided a place to stay and work while this project was realized, and especially the veterans who participated in this project.

The Addison Gallery of American Art is a department of Phillips Academy

© Addison Gallery of American Art
All rights reserved
Phillips Academy, Andover, MA 01810

ISB Number: 1–879886–32–4
Library of Congress Catalog Number 91–78029

★ This book is dedicated to the memory of Clarence Fitch

Photography
_____

William Short

Design
_____

Sally Roy Abugov, Office of Publications

Printing
_____

LaVigne Press